UNDERSTANDING THE UNDERCLASS

Informing policy by establishing facts

The Policy Studies Institute (PSI) is Britain's leading independent research organisation undertaking studies of economic, industrial and social policy, and the workings of political institutions.

PSI is a registered charity, run on a non-profit basis, and is not associated with any political party, pressure group or commercial interest.

PSI attaches great importance to covering a wide range of subject areas with its multi-disciplinary approach. The Institute's 40+ researchers are organised in teams which currently cover the following programmes:

Family Finances and Social Security
Health Studies and Social Care
Innovation and New Technology
Quality of Life and the Environment
Social Justice and Social Order
Employment Studies
Arts and the Cultural Industries
Information Policy
Education

This publication arises from the Social Justice and Social Order programme and is one of over 30 publications made available by the Institute each year.

Information about the work of PSI, and a catalogue of available books can be obtained from:

Marketing Department, PSI
100 Park Village East, London NW1 3SR

UNDERSTANDING THE UNDERCLASS

Edited by
DAVID J. SMITH

POLICY STUDIES INSTITUTE
100 PARK VILLAGE EAST, LONDON NWI 3SR

The publishing imprint of the independent
POLICY STUDIES INSTITUTE
100 Park Village East, London NW1 3SR
Telephone: 071-387 2171; Fax: 071-388 0914

ISBN 0 85374 538 2

A CIP catalogue record of this book is available from the British Library.

1 2 3 4 5 6 7 8 9

How to obtain PSI publications
All book shop and individual orders should be sent to PSI's distributors:

BEBC Ltd
9 Albion Close, Parkstone, Poole, Dorset, BH12 3LL

Books will normally be despatched in 24 hours. Cheques should be made payable to BEBC Ltd.

Credit card and telephone/fax orders may be placed on the following freephone numbers:

FREEPHONE: 0800 262260   FREEFAX: 0800 262266

Booktrade Representation (UK & Eire)
Book Representation Ltd
P O Box 17, Canvey Island, Essex SS8 8HZ

PSI Subscriptions
PSI Publications are available on subscription.
Further information from PSI's subscription agent:

Carfax Publishing Company Ltd
Abingdon Science Park, P O Box 25, Abingdon OX10 3UE

Laserset by Policy Studies Institute
Printed in Great Britain by Billings & Sons Ltd, Worcester

Contents

Preface

This volume brings together the papers given at a conference on 26 February 1991 at the Policy Studies Institute on *the idea of an underclass in Britain.* Funding for the conference and for the preparation of this volume was generously provided by the Joseph Rowntree Foundation. We are grateful to Professor Michael Rutter, who skilfully chaired the day's proceedings.

The background to the conference was a sudden increase in discussion about the idea that there might be a growing underclass in Britain, stimulated to a large extent by writers belonging to the political Right. This led to a wholesale rejection of the concept by a number of academic writers on social policy, who wished to dissociate themselves from an idea they saw as a tool for the repression of the poor. At a seminar at the Institute of Economic Affairs in 1990, the American writer, Charles Murray, who had foreseen the emergence of an underclass in Britain, and Professor Alan Walker, a member of the British social policy establishment, staked out their positions and fought a pitched battle.

The clash of views about social policy was genuine enough, but it was passionately held views about policy which dictated the social analysis rather than the other way about. The general purpose of the PSI conference was to reverse the direction of thought: to start with analysis and evidence, then move towards policy. A summary of the first chapter on *defining the underclass* was circulated to speakers well in advance; and they were asked to address the idea of an underclass as set out in that chapter.

Chapters 2 and 3 present the results of new analyses of the Labour Force Survey, the British Social Attitudes Survey, and the British Election Survey, which test the evidence on the existence, size, and nature of an underclass on the proposed definition. Chapters 4 and 5 are discussions of theories and explanations of an underclass, from differing political perspectives. Chapters 6 and 7, by leading members of think-tanks of the Left and Right respectively, discuss policy implications. Somewhat predictably, the discussion drifts further and further away from the proposed definition as we move from hard-nosed analysis of survey data, through discussion of theory, to policy prescriptions.

It was not finally possible to stick to a single, simple, notion of what the underclass is or might be; but the strategy did at least produce a cool and constructive discussion. Chapter 8 summarises the main points made at the conference itself, and prepares the way for a fuller investigation of this subject which, despite the wishes of some of the conference participants, will probably not go away.

1

The contributors

Nick Buck is Chief Research Officer at the ESRC Research Centre on Micro-Social Change at Essex University.

James Cornford is Director of the Institute for Public Policy Research.

Sir Ralf Dahrendorf is Warden of St Antony's College, Oxford.

David G. Green is Director of the Health and Welfare Unit at the Institute of Economic Affairs.

Anthony Heath is a Fellow of Nuffield College, Oxford.

David J. Smith is a Senior Fellow and Head of the Social Justice Programme at the Policy Studies Institute.

David Willetts is Director of the Centre for Policy Studies.

1 Defining the Underclass

David J. Smith

As Karl Popper has repeatedly pointed out, there is not usually any need to define our terms. Serious discussion is about ideas, theories, and facts: never merely about words. Most of the time we understand what people mean well enough for the purpose of debate. A clearer understanding of the concepts in play is an outcome of discussion rather than a pre-condition.

However, there is currently a special problem about the use of the term *underclass*, especially since there is disagreement about whether it should be used at all. Although it has been widely used by sociologists, including for example Giddens and Runciman, and although it was used in the 1960s by thinkers belonging to the Left to analyse the marginal position of racial minorities in South Africa and in Britain, more recently the idea of an underclass has been deployed most prominently by the new Right in debates about American social policy. In this context, the idea of an underclass is closely wedded to a social and political theory, and implicitly or explicitly connected with a political programme belonging to the radical Right. In Charles Murray's writings, for example, a growing American underclass is seen as the pathological manifestation of a culture of dependency created by social welfare policies. As it is the Right that has been making the running in this debate, alternative views, for example that the phenomenon is caused by a failure of economic and labour market policy, are identified much less closely with the underclass idea. The response of some writers who do not belong to the Right has been to reject altogether the use of a term which they think has been appropriated, or misappropriated, by their political opponents.

The PSI conference is intended to promote serious discussion of this issue among people holding different political views. To make that discussion possible, there has to be a working agreement about the use of the term *underclass*.

As a broad strategy, it is proposed that theories, explanations and valuations should not be allowed to shape our central conception of what the underclass is. If there is to be a useful discussion among people holding different political views, the underclass cannot be *defined* as a group characterised by a culture of dependency, or as the undeserving poor. Instead, a culture of dependency would be an idea that some introduce to elaborate a description of the underclass, or to explain why this group exists and grows; others could reject that characterisation of the group and that explanation of its existence and growth without having to deny that an underclass exists.

3

The advantage of this strategy is that it makes a discussion possible. The particular advantage for those on the Left is that it allows them to develop a reply to the theories of the new Right, rather than retreating behind a ban on the use of the term.

It is therefore proposed that we should adopt a minimalist approach to saying what is essentially meant by an underclass. At a minimum, the idea of an underclass is a counterpart to the idea of social classes, and acquires its meaning within that same framework of analysis.

The modern idea of social class, as distinct from older conceptions of rank, station, blood, and breeding, derives from Marx, who emphasised the relationship with the mode of production as the source of class distinctions. Sociologists argue about whether social classes are antagonistic groups which differ in a variety of ways, or a series of groups ordered in a neat hierarchy on a single dimension, such as prestige, authority, or pay. Still, sociologists all tend to use a similar class schema, regardless of where they stand on the theoretical issue, and this schema is a compromise between the two opposing views. The array of social classes does tend to approximate towards a hierarchy in wholly industrial or post-industrial societies[1] yet different classes do have different kinds of relationship with productive employment, and this lies at the heart of the distinctions that are made.

The underclass are those who fall outside this class schema, because they belong to family units having no stable relationship at all with the 'mode of production' – with legitimate gainful employment.[2] If the social classes are viewed as a hierarchical array, then the underclass lies outside the schema, and beneath the bottom class. There is a clear need for such a category within the original Marxist schema, and equally within the modern conception of social class which inclines more towards an occupational hierarchy. Recognising this, Marx himself, of course, used the contemptuous term 'lumpenproletariat' to describe what we would call the underclass today. His use of the term emphasises the close connection between analysis and explanatory or normative theories. In these respects, Marx and Charles Murray are very much alike. Nevertheless, for the purpose of analysis alone, there is a need for an underclass category to supplement the social class schema – if there are families which do not have a stable relationship with legitimate employment.

A modern exposition of this general view is given in an article on social class by W.G. Runciman.[3] Runciman describes classes as sets of roles defined by the nature and degree of economic power attaching to them through their relation to the processes of production, distribution and exchange. Because the paid work that people do is the most obvious determinant of their life chances, the most important roles are occupational. Where people perform no occupational role, their social class must be decided by an assessment of the economic power attaching to the roles they do perform. Where the same person performs several roles (for example, as wife of a salaried professional and as typist) a decision must be made as to which role is more important in determining the person's economic power. A household role may often outweigh an occupational one. Starting from this conception of the idea of social classes, Runciman deduces that there is also an underclass.

> That there is below the two working classes an underclass which constitutes a separate category of roles is ... readily demonstrable... But the term must be understood to stand not for a group or category of workers systematically disadvantaged within the labour market..., but for those members of British society whose roles place them more or less permanently at the economic level where benefits are paid by the state to those unable to participate in the labour market at all. This, admittedly, does not prevent some of them from having incomes from the state higher than they could earn in regular employment...[4]

Stability of underclass membership

Empirical studies show that social class is something fundamental that strongly influences the whole range of social and economic relationships. To put the point crudely, anything at all analysed by social class will show large and consistent differences. This is possible only because there is a considerable degree of stability of class membership. People move only slowly and with difficulty from one social class to another during their lifetimes, and there is a considerable degree of class stability between generations. If class membership becomes more fluid, then cultural differences between social classes tend to diminish.

Within the framework proposed here, social classes are defined by reference to economic power, not cultural differences. People continue to belong to distinct social classes depending on their economic power even where there is a high degree of social mobility and consequently a reduction in cultural differences between classes.[5] The extent of cultural differences between classes is therefore a matter for empirical study, not a part of the idea of social class. However, empirical studies do show that the cultural differences between social classes are large and all-embracing; and the existence of these cultural differences makes the idea of social class, essential to the understanding of most aspects of social life.

The idea of an underclass only makes sense if there is some degree of stability in its membership, because the underclass are defined as 'those unable to participate in the labour market at all'. There could be a fairly large group of people who are out of work at any one time, but no substantial group of people who are usually out of work. In that case, there would be no underclass: only a working class, some of whom are temporarily out of work.

On the other hand, inter-generational stability does not seem to be part of the core meaning of 'class' or 'underclass'. Modern studies have shown that social classes continue to exist, and to have fundamental importance, even when there is a high level of upward mobility between generations (as the upper classes grow in size relative to the lower classes). The test of stability applied to an underclass need be no tougher than that applied to a class.

Secondary labour market

It may be suggested that people belonging to a secondary labour market in which jobs offer poor security and low pay, and are often part-time, also belong to an underclass. However, there are good reasons for not extending the concept in this way. First, there would be great difficulty in arriving at a clear definition of the 'secondary labour market'. Second, many jobs in what is commonly thought of as the secondary labour market are also a secondary source of income for the family unit, so that the people doing these jobs are often not in a precarious situation.

What remains open

This account of what is meant by the idea of an underclass as far as possible leaves the field open for competing theories, explanations, and prescriptions. The following are among the questions that remain open and that may be pursued by contributors to the PSI conference.

The existence and size of an underclass

Whether there are family units having no stable relationship with legitimate gainful employment depends on whether there is a group that stays out of work for very long periods. It also depends on the criterion of stability – or length of time out of employment – that is adopted. No particular criterion will be proposed here: conference participants will want to put forward their own views on this point.

Secular trends
On the type of definition proposed, an underclass could grow in size, or diminish and even disappear. Information on secular trends is particularly important, since a number of writers (both on the right and on the left) have taken as a starting point the proposition that the underclass is growing in size.

Composition of an underclass
Given a definition along the lines proposed, the composition of the underclass will be a matter for empirical research. Important points are the proportion of the underclass who are lone, never-married mothers, divorced or separated women, and couples at various stages of the life cycle.

Poverty
On the type of definition proposed, the underclass are not the same as the poor, and the debate about an underclass is not a re-run of earlier debates about where to draw the poverty line. How many of the underclass are poor, and how many of the poor belong to the underclass, become questions to be answered by empirical research.

Ecology
American thinking (both liberal and conservative) has strongly emphasised ecological effects in seeking to explain the growth of an underclass. According to William Julius Wilson, for example, the underclass grows because middle class black people (partly because of affirmative action policies) move away from inner city areas of high black concentration, so that these areas become dominated by people having no stable relationship with the main economic and social order, and enter a downward spiral. Against the background of such theories, it is important to establish how far the underclass are in fact concentrated within restricted areas in sharp decline. On the type of definition proposed this is, of course, a matter for empirical research, since the underclass are not *defined* as people living in certain areas. Area analysis may then be used to address the theoretical question whether, as Wilson believes, concentration effects explain a growth in the underclass.

Citizenship and participation
Poverty has often been explained as inability to participate at a minimum level in the common culture. More recently, the idea of citizenship has been invoked by some to explain what is meant by an underclass. On this view the underclass are that group of people who are not fully citizens because they are not able to participate in certain basic social activities. Citizenship and participation do not enter into the kind of definition of the underclass that is proposed here. The extent to which the underclass do participate in the common culture and play their part as citizens therefore becomes a matter for empirical research.

Work motivation and social responsibility
Some writers believe that members of the underclass are not motivated to work and do not accept responsibility for themselves or for the consequences of their actions. It may be that some regard this as the defining characteristic of the underclass. A possible reading of Charles Murray, for example, is that the underclass is defined by a culture that devalues work and social responsibility; and that it is because of this culture that

members of the underclass have no stable employment and tend to be poor. On the type of analysis proposed here, however, culture is not the defining characteristic; so the level of work motivation and social responsibility of the underclass is something that demands to be investigated by empirical research.

Exclusion and self-exclusion
It can be argued that the underclass are excluded from the mainstream of society, for example because there is a mismatch between the skills and qualifications that they can conceivably obtain and the job opportunities available to them.[6] Against this, it can be argued that members of the underclass exclude themselves by refusing to make the best of their opportunities. The suggested definition leaves the field open for these two types of explanation to be tested against the evidence.

Family structure
The suggested definition assumes that the basic economic unit is the small family group. Hence, the underclass is not individuals who have no stable relationship with legitimate gainful employment, but members of family units that have no such relationship. It follows that the structure of family units must have far-reaching consequences for the size and nature of an underclass. There will be a strong tendency for single parents of young children to belong to the underclass. Single parenthood is no part of the suggested definition of the underclass: many single parents would not be members of the underclass, and many members of the underclass would not be single parents. On the other hand, a growth in single parenthood could well be an important explanation of a growth in the underclass.

Structure versus culture
Underlying much of the debate about the underclass is a contest between structure and culture as the determinant of social developments. On the one hand there is the view that changes in economic structure (such as the reduction in the number of simple manual jobs on offer), institutional structures (such as poor education and training provision especially in declining urban areas) and the lack of appropriate facilities (such as nursery schools accessible to single mothers) deny a section of the population the opportunity and resources to compete for jobs. On the other hand there is the view that these people have lost the will to compete by virtue of the culture to which they belong (although it may also be argued that this culture is itself partly the result of structures and institutions, such as the state welfare system). It is because the idea of an underclass has become associated with cultural explanations that some people on the Left have thought that any use of the term is equivalent to 'blaming the victim'.

Within the framework here proposed, the idea of an underclass is *defined* in structural terms, but this says nothing about the reasons for the growth of an underclass in some modern societies. It is perfectly possible to argue that cultural factors (such as attitudes to work or marriage and childbearing) ultimately determine people's economic power and consign some to the underclass, without *defining* the underclass by reference to attitudes. Equally, of course, to deploy the idea of an underclass in the sense here proposed is not to endorse a cultural explanation.

Perhaps more fruitfully, the proposed idea of an underclass allows for the possibility that structure and culture interact, and that the priority between them cannot be decided.

Why a growing underclass would matter

Whether there is a growing underclass in Britain is a matter for empirical investigation. To raise the question is not to voice a moral panic that carries its own agenda with it.

A growing underclass in Britain would, however, be a profoundly important part of the social scene, which would need to be considered when deciding policy in many fields, including labour market policy, education, family policy, state welfare systems, housing, social services, and crime prevention. There would be a moral imperative to do whatever can be done to reduce the number of people with no power and no stake in the economic system. At the same time, the majority have an interest in preventing the growth of a group which already causes them inconvenience, and might eventually threaten the stability of economic and social institutions.[7]

Notes

1. Not in societies at an earlier stage of development, because agricultural workers and industrial workers clearly belong to different classes, but have an indefinite relationship to each other in a hierarchy of authority or prestige.
2. Old age pensioners are not included: they have a stable historic relationship with legitimate employment, which is recognised and continued through the payment of their pension. The definition is in terms of family units, because these are the relevant economic entities; hence adult dependants do not normally belong to the underclass. People living on accumulated or inherited capital do not belong to the underclass; like pensioners, they benefit from a historic relationship with the mode of production.
3. W.G. Runciman, 'How Many Classes are There in Contemporary British Society?', *Sociology*, 24.3 (1990).
4. Runciman, p.388.
5. Again, this is in agreement with Runciman's view.
6. It is sometimes argued that the idea of exclusion implies agency, and that no-one has performed an act of exclusion in this case. The reply would be that the underclass are excluded as a result of political acts that might have been otherwise and to which we have all consented.
7. This is to take the opposite view from Marx, who blamed the *lumpenproletariat* for preventing the revolution: see F. Bovenkerk, 'The Rehabilitation of the Rabble: How and Why Marx and Engels Wrongly Depicted the Lumpenproletariat as a Reactionary Force', *The Netherlands Journal of Sociology*, 20.1 (1984).

2 Labour Market Inactivity and Polarisation
A household perspective on the idea of an underclass*

Nick Buck

Introduction

Economic changes in Britain in the 1970s and 1980s have had a major impact on the distribution of resources and life chances in society. From around the early 1970s a combination of government policy, de-industrialisation and demographic change have led to a significant increase in levels of unemployment, compared with what had been experienced in most of the first three decades since the Second World War. Employment growth was sluggish up to the early 1980s, and growth since then has been polarised between high-wage non-manual jobs and part-time, generally low-wage jobs mainly filled by women. Combined with a more general occupational restructuring, this has led to a significant dispersion of labour market earnings. Together with the effects of rising unemployment, and particularly the polarisation between work-rich and work-poor households, these factors have contributed to a very substantial increase in household income inequality during the 1980s.[1] These income disparities did not reduce with declining unemployment in the later 1980s, and the polarisation of income and work at the household level appears to have persisted.

As one aspect of this polarisation, it has been suggested that we have in Britain an emerging underclass of people, who are excluded, or exclude themselves, from many of the material benefits of society, and whose exclusion depends to a substantial degree on their non-participation in the labour market.[2] Some of these theories also describe other forms of behaviour as characteristic of members of the underclass, and Murray, at least, argues that the growth of illegitimate births and of criminal behaviour have, independently of detachment from the labour market, caused the underclass to grow. A different argument that has been put forward from the perspective of social class theory is that any class stratification schema needs to take into account the existence of an underclass, defined by a more or less permanent inability to participate in the labour market.[3]

* The support of the Economic and Social Research Council (ESRC) is gratefully acknowledged. The work was part of the programme of the ESRC Research Centre on Micro-Social Change in Britain. The data from Labour Force Survey was supplied by the the Office of Population Censuses and Surveys through the ESRC Data Archive. Neither of these bodies bears any responsibility for the analysis reported here, or for the conclusions reached.

This chapter explores how far it is possible to identify and measure an underclass from available data on labour market behaviour. It therefore relates to economic definitions of the underclass, and has nothing to say about other possible definitions. It presents an analysis of economic activity at the household or family level, focusing particularly on households with no labour market activity, measuring how their numbers have changed during the 1980s, and what characteristics they possess.

The way in which the evidence is marshalled in this chapter is thus driven by David Smith's suggestions in Chapter 1. The objective is to explore how far existing statistics allow us to identify and measure 'family units having no stable relationship at all ... with legitimate gainful employment'. The analysis is also informed by his perspective of seeing the underclass as analogous to social classes, which implies that similar criteria or tests for stability of membership are applicable.

This chapter then has a mainly descriptive aim; it is not for the most part concerned with explanations of the existence or growth of an underclass. However, because there is a necessary interaction between definition, explanation and measurement, some further clarification will be necessary. In particular this introduction briefly discusses two themes: the context for the development of the idea of an underclass; and more specifically the macro-economic and labour market context, and the notions of stability and permanence which are central to any definition.

Development of the idea of an underclass

The idea that there were strata at the bottom of society which had to be classified in a different manner from the rest of the social structure, and which could not be defined as some fraction of the working class, has considerable longevity. It was for example shared across a wide spectrum of social thought in Victorian Britain. It was at the heart of debates in this period about how to deal with poverty and with unemployment.[4] Although this tradition of thought identified the problems as being caused by individual behaviour, it led to increased state intervention, rather than reliance on market processes. The particular context for the development of concerns about the 'dangerous classes', or about an unemployable fraction of the population, was the casual labour market of the large cities, and particularly London. These concerns were associated with unstable labour markets, within which a lowest stratum was seen to earn a tenuous living through occasional work, dependence on public poor relief and private charity, and in a minority of cases criminal behaviour. Surprisingly, the underlying concept does not seem to have been so salient in policy debate during conditions of long-term unemployment experienced in the inter-war period.

Current uses of the term underclass in Britain have been explicitly related to recent usage in the United States. The context for this American usage is significant and has implications for the applicability of the term in Britain. After recession in the early 1980s which led to significant increases in unemployment and poverty, a period of sustained growth occurred. The problem was that this growth did not seem to be reducing poverty or chronic unemployment for significant subsections of the population. A plethora of explanations have been advanced for this, and the problem has been defined in a number of distinct ways. Broadly there has been a division between explanations in terms of structure and in terms of individual behaviour. Structural explanations have focused on a mismatch between jobs and potential workers; this mismatch might be spatial or occupational or both. By contrast, the behavioural explanations seek to explain patterns of dependency in terms of rational choice models, social psychological models and cultural models.[5] What has been particularly distinctive about the American economic experience, compared to that of Britain, and much of Europe, has been the very much higher levels of job creation, and in particular a much greater growth of low-wage jobs and jobs with poor security. Greater wage flexibility probably has led to less chronic unemployment than in European countries, but to more poor-quality jobs, and more people subsisting on unstable or marginal forms of employment.

Economic policy responses in Britain in the 1980s have been rather different. In spite of attempts to increase wage flexibility and to use unemployment as a labour market discipline, other policies have tended to preserve and enhance the standard of living of those in employment; for example, the downward pressure on wages of excess labour supply has been reduced by encouraging early retirement and by adopting, at least up to mid-1980s, a relatively permissive approach to payment of social assistance to the long-term unemployed. Consequently, if we are to find an underclass in Britain, it is likely to be constituted in different ways from that in the US: to be characterised more by persistent long-term unemployment than by occasional work or participation in non-legitimate forms of employment.

Definition of stability and permanence

This discussion raises the question how the working definition of a potential underclass – those families which do not have a stable relationship with legitimate gainful employment – should be elaborated. At issue in particular are issues of stability and duration. It is not pedantic to distinguish between a stable *absence* of relationship to legitimate employment on the one hand, and an unstable relationship *with* employment on the other. The use of the term both in Victorian discussion of the casual poor and in contemporary discussion in the US relates more to unstable relationships to employment rather than a total absence of relationship. The second problem is how either definition should be operationalised. For example in the case of the 'stable underclass', what period of labour market inactivity should determine potential membership? Should such inactivity be seen as equally significant under all conditions?

A framework for posing these questions is in terms of the risks and chances which individuals and families face in economic and social life. Clearly everyone faces uncertainty in maintaining a standard of living. Jobs may be lost, attempts to move to a better job may fail, divorce and separation can result in a substantial decline in real income, particularly for women, and sickness and accidents may reduce earning potential. These risks are structured very unequally. Some types of jobs are very much more insecure than others, the probability of illness and accident are very much higher among working class families than among middle class families. Correspondingly the chances of leaving a situation of poverty, disadvantage or unemployment once it is entered vary substantially.

The risks of downward and upward mobility, and in particular entering or leaving a situation of disadvantage are partly independent of one another, since the mechanisms by which people enter and leave are different. Both however will depend on household and individual characteristics and the economic and social contexts in which individuals and families find themselves. It is important to see this type of model dynamically, since these probabilities can be subject to change over time, and as a result of previous experience. Past experience of unemployment for example is likely to increase the risks of unemployment.

Thus a simple model for viewing dynamically the idea of an underclass defined in terms of stable relationship with legitimate employment could be framed in terms of probabilities of entering or leaving non-employment. One is still left with a distinction between an underclass defined on the one hand as those with a very low probability of leaving non-employment once they enter that state, and those with a significant probability of leaving non-employment, but with a very high probability of re-entering this state.

For the whole population both these probabilities are strongly influenced by the state of the national economy, by rises and falls in national unemployment, so that proportions who fall into our definition of a potential underclass will vary cyclically over time. Similarly the probabilities of entering or leaving economic inactivity are, as we shall see below, strongly related to stages in the life cycle. This raises problems if we are using the term underclass in a manner consonant with that of social class, since some notion of stability of membership over time and over the life cycle is usually implied. If membership of the group is essentially tied in this way to economic conditions and to life cycle stage, then the phenomenon would certainly present very considerable policy problems but it might not be appropriate to define it as a detached fraction of the population with anything like the stability of social classes.

Unfortunately there does not exist at present any data representative of the general population of Britain which would allow us to assess movements over the long term in and out of the labour market. What would be necessary for this would be longitudinal data on work experience covering a decade or more, which could allow us to identify how far past experience affected future prospects, and how far there was a distinct stratum whose movements were much less susceptible to changes in national economic conditions than other parts of the population. In the absence of this data this paper relies on cross-sectional data on the current labour market state, along with some measure of how long individuals have remained in this state. The next section briefly introduces these data and the methods of analysis used.

Data and methods
Much of the analysis in this paper is based on the Labour Force Survey. This is a large scale national sample survey, carried out biennially up to 1983, and annually from then on. Its coverage is mainly of labour market behaviour, as well as housing, education and training. One of its particular advantages for our purposes is that its basic sampling unit is the household, and it provides full information on all household members. It thus allows an analysis of the relationships between the labour market situation of different household members, and of individual work situations in different types of family and household. Its other major advantage is the very large sample size, in excess of 60,000 households since 1983, and more than 80,000 before then.

The following section is based on a comparative analysis of the survey micro-data sets for 1979 and 1986. The former year was around the peak of the relatively weak economic up-turn of the late 1970s, while 1986 was the year in which registered unemployment peaked after a substantial rise in the early 1980s, though gross domestic product had been growing three years previously to this. Ideally one would also want to compare a more recent survey after registered unemployment had fallen significantly, but the relevant micro-data sets are not yet available.

The basic unit of analysis for our purpose should be a narrowly defined family unit. However there are difficulties in implementing this with the 1979 data, and the major part of the analysis is based on using households. defined as those sharing accommodation.[6] In 1986 the narrowly-defined family unit was identifiable, and some results are presented on this base. The rationale for using the family rather than the individual is that at least in principle it is a unit within which resources are shared[7] and within which labour market participation decisions of separate members are likely to interact. For many purposes state welfare systems also treat the family as the basic unit for the assessment of needs, resources and entitlements.

However this raises problems of how family labour market activity can be used as a concept, given that except in family businesses, labour market activity is essentially an individual concept. The two solutions would be to treat one key individual as being dominant in the definition of the family's activity or to provide a measure which summarises some or all family members' activities. Where we are using family labour market activity as a measure of social position this raises problems of how legitimate it is to base a categorisation of an individual's social position on that of other household members. There are then problems essentially similar to those confronted when assigning social class to members of couples. The problem is how we are to arrive at a measure of household labour market activity on the basis of the activity of individual household members. The difficulty within couples is that to use a key individual (for example, Goldthorpe's definition of the partner 'whose labour market participation may be regarded as dominant') without much fuller information on earnings potential and other measures of dominance than is usually available, will mean that the male partner will almost necessarily be selected. However it is difficult to see why a couple household should be regarded as economically active if the husband is working and the wife is not, but not in the reverse situation. The evidence is here presented in most of the tables in two ways: first, classifying by the husband's status in married couple households (labelled the 'household head' basis); and second, classifying by the status of the more active of the partners whichever this is (labelled the 'joint activity' basis). In the case of working adult children I have presented some evidence on their prevalence in 'inactive' households, but have not treated them as contributing to the household activity definition. This may create some limited distortions, particularly in the case of older lone-parent families.

As suggested above it was not readily possible to adjust the 1979 data to narrowly defined family units. However in 1986 it is possible to distinguish family units within households. As defined here family units comprise people related by marriage (or cohabitation) and their children. However children of other household members who are themselves married or have children constitute separate family units. Unrelated people, or people otherwise related to other household members (for example, brothers or sisters) will also form separate units. There are thus only four different types of family unit: single individuals, couples without children, couples with children and lone parent families. The data for 1986 are presented on both a household and a family unit basis.

David Smith has suggested that pensioners should be excluded from the potential underclass, on the basis that they have a stable historic relationship to legitimate employment. In this paper I have excluded individuals not of working age. However it is clear from analyses of income distribution that pensioners, and particularly lone pensioners contain one of the largest groups in poverty in Britain. Moreover in Runciman's definition it is not clear why pensioners dependent on social security benefits should not be included, on the basis that they do not have adequate wealth or pension rights arising from their participation in paid employment. To explore this further would require different types of data.

The distribution of labour market activity in British households

The interaction of household structure and individual labour market activity is critical to this analysis, which therefore begins by summarising LFS data for 1979 and 1986 on the distribution of work situations within families. The analysis in this section is restricted to households with a main (potential) earner of working age. The first step is to distinguish between three different economic activity situations for individuals: being in employment, being unemployed (in the sense of looking for work) for less than a year, and all other situations, including having been seeking work for more than a year. The assumption is that the last group contains, though it is not identical with, some potential underclass based on long term detachment from the labour market. It does not of course necessarily coincide with an underclass defined by unstable attachment.

The presentation is somewhat complex since there are four dimensions of interest, as well as time; the type of household, the work situation of the 'head', the work situation of the 'wife' if any, and the work situation of any adult children. Table 2.1 shows the changing distribution of households by type.[8] In 1979 approximately 15 per cent of households consisted of one person only, whilst households containing couples accounted for 76 per cent of households, with 52 per cent containing children. Lone-parent households made up 7.5 per cent of the total, of which around a third contained only children over 16. By 1986 the proportion of households containing couples had declined to 72 per cent, but there were shifts within this group and the couples with older children only had increased significantly. The proportion of lone-parent families had increased to nearly 9 per cent, with again the sharpest increase in the families with older children. As suggested above, changing household definitions confuse the picture for single-person and other household types. On the basis of family units the distribution by family type is rather different: single person family units account for a significantly higher proportion of families, lone-parent families account for a marginally higher proprotion, while couple-based families account for only 67 per cent. The significance of the changes is clearer when we look at the distribution of economic activity by household type, since this varies so substantially.

Table 2.2 shows the work situation of the primary (potential) earner in each of these household types in 1979. It shows that there were very much higher employment rates and very much higher activity rates in couple households compared with the other types. There are marginal variations between the different types of couple households, with higher activity amongst those with younger children, somewhat lower activity amongst those with older children, and lower activity still amongst those without children. These differences seem most likely to arise from differences in life-cycle stage. A later analysis will show that, after controlling for age, the effect of increasing numbers of children is to reduce activity rates. Single-person households had a substantially lower activity rate, while lone-parent households had a lower activity rate still. However among these lone parents, there are sharp differences by life-cycle stage, with much higher activity rates among those with older children. In general the proportion unemployed for less than a year varies between household types in parallel with the proportion inactive; the highest proportion seeking work and the highest proportion inactive are both found amongst lone parents with young children. These facts conflict with the theory that there is a polarisation between household types which are attached to and detached from the labour market.

These data suggest however that changes in the distribution by household type would have led to an increase in the overall inactivity rate, if the rates for each household type had remained the same, since the proportion of low activity household types was tending to rise. However, the total effect would be small. It certainly would not account for the increase between 1979 and 1986 in the proportion who were inactive, as shown by Table 2.3. As a proportion of all working-age households this group increased from 12.5 per cent to 20.5 per cent. This substantial increase affected all household types. The *increment* in the proportion of households that were inactive was greatest amongst 'younger' lone-parent families, couples without children and couples with older children. Excepting the miscellaneous 'other household' category, the increase was lowest amongst 'older' lone-parent families. However, the *rate* of increase was greatest amongst couple households, and particularly those with younger children.

However this pattern is complicated somewhat when we consider the relationship between husbands' and wives' work situations in couple households.[9] Table 2.4 examines this interaction for 1979 and 1986. It shows very clearly the polarisation of work within households to which Pahl has referred.[10] Overall, married women's employment rate and participation rate have grown over this period, but this masks a substantial *increase* in the proportion of the wives of *employed* husbands who are working, and a *decline* in the activity rate of wives of long-term *unemployed* and *inactive* husbands. Interestingly, the wives of shorter-term unemployed husbands have seen a growth in activity rate which is much closer to the employed than to the inactive. However even given this polarisation there is a substantial minority of households which might be classified as inactive on the basis of the husband's work situation, but not on the basis of the wife's.

In 1979 there were 807,000 households containing employed adult children, or 22 per cent of all households containing children aged over 16. By 1986 the number had risen to 919,000 and the proportion to 23 per cent. The great majority of these were in households where at least one parent was working. However in 1979 the proportions of working adult children in inactive households were not significantly lower than in the general population, accounting for 26 per cent of the relevant couple households and 19 per cent of relevant lone parent families. By 1986 these proportions had fallen, to 21 per cent for couple households and to 16 per cent for lone parent families. The definition of household activity has not been modified to reflect adult children's employment.

Table 2.5 summarises the analysis so far by showing estimated numbers of inactive and long-term unemployed households. In terms of distribution by household type, in 1979 single-person households were 41 per cent of inactive households, couple households were 29 per cent and lone-parent households were 27 per cent (all figures are on a joint activity basis). This is clearly very sharply different from the distribution of these types in the general population. However changes by 1986 involved a much greater growth in inactive couple households than the other groups, and their share of inactive households had risen to 40 per cent. This was still well short of their population share.

However the long-term unemployed and inactive population discussed so far includes a number of groups which should not be included in any potential underclass. The three groups at issue are the early retired, the long-term sick and students. On the basis of the 'no stable relationship' definition one may want to argue that those who retire early should be treated in the same way as the retired of pensionable age, in the sense that their social position still depends on their historic relationship to the labour market. Similar arguments may apply to some of the long-term sick, though this raises greater problems since some of this group may never have had any stable relationship with employment. On Runciman's definition of the underclass, whether these groups should be included will depend on whether or not they depend exclusively on state benefits, presumably excluding contributory pensions which derive from past labour market participation. The case of students is rather different, since they are likely to have a prospective involvement in the labour market. There seems to be no reason for including them within any possible definition of the underclass. All three groups are excluded from the following analyses, although some members might plausibly be included depending on the precise definition of the underclass that is adopted.

Table 2.6 shows the same categories as Table 2.5, but excluding the above groups. The differences are substantial. The total number of households covered falls from 1.7 million to 0.7 million (or 4.4 per cent of all households) in 1979, and from 2.8 million to 1.6 million (or 10.5 per cent of all households) in 1986. The rate of growth of these remaining groups is however then more than twice as great as that in the broad definition. The concentration by household type is also affected substantially: in 1979 lone-parent families constituted 56 per cent of all inactive households on the narrow definition. However the difference in rates of change by household type are also magnified. While the number of inactive lone-parent families grew by less than 40 per cent, the number of inactive couple households grew by 350 per cent, and their share of all inactive households grew from 20 per cent to 38 per cent.

The estimated total population in these households grew from 1.96 million in 1979 (or 4.2 per cent of the total population in working age households) to 4.58 million (9.9 per cent of the total population).[11] An interesting observation arises from the separate household and family unit analysis for 1986, since this allows the identification of concealed families, that is family units living within households whose type is defined by another family unit. The great majority of these are single persons, but there are also an estimated 310,000 concealed couples and 164,000 concealed lone-parent families. The analysis of activity rates for these concealed families separately suggests significant differences from main family households of the same type. In summary, for single-person households and one-parent families, the activity rates in concealed families are higher than for equivalent main family units. However husbands in concealed couples have lower activity rates. Wives' activity rates on the other hand are higher than average, after controlling for husband's activity. There are equivalent gender differences for the other two household types, with female lone parents and female single persons having a relatively higher activity rate in concealed compared to main households, while for men there is either no difference or the activity rate is lower. This evidence suggests that the social support available in extended families provides women with the opportunity to work, while for men it seems to provide the opportunity not to work.

The evidence presented so far is based on answers to survey questions about labour market status. There clearly should be some question over the reliability of some of this data. For example, what do respondents count as work for pay? How far are their answers about job search conditioned by the knowledge that this may be a condition of receiving benefits? There is also clearly a major problem of discouraged workers – those who are not looking for work on the (possibly realistic) basis that in current labour market conditions they are unlikely to be able to find a job. Similarly some may not be looking on the basis that current family responsibilities would prevent them taking the sorts of jobs likely to be available given the childcare facilities or care facilities for other family members that they could use. In different circumstances, they may well look for work. Defining either of these groups as permanently out of the labour market may be inaccurate. The LFS carries some information on the reasons why respondents are not looking for work: the results are shown for the long-term unemployed and inactive households (based on household head) Table 2.7. Comparisons over time are very unreliable here, in part because the form of questions changed. Fewer people are likely to have been classified to the 'other inactive' category in 1979 and it is not possible to distinguish those in this category who say they would like work, even though they are not looking. The estimate of growth in this category shown in the table is likely to be excessive, but undoubtedly the number of 'discouraged workers', that is those who are not looking for work because they believe no jobs are available, is likely to have increased substantially given the increase in the overall level of unemployment. However when this category is grouped with those looking after a family, the combined group has grown more slowly than the long-term unemployed. On the evidence only of those looking after a family (who are mainly lone parents), the proportion which does not want work has not grown. On the other hand, assuming that the two groups were confused in 1979, and that the other inactive in 1979 were divided as they were in 1986, then the number not wanting work may have grown by up to 80 per cent, more slowly than the total of inactive households.

Correlates of labour market inactivity

So far this chapter has considered the numbers of households of various types which appear to have a weak relationship to the labour market. This second part of the analysis explores the other characteristics of households weakly attached to the labour market, in particular their spatial distribution, and the characteristics of their heads of household. The results of an analysis of variance in household inactivity are summarised in Tables 2.8 and 2.9. Household inactivity in 1979 (Table 2.8) and 1986 (Table 2.9) is defined in terms of household head status, with students, the long-term sick and the retired excluded. The tables show in the first column the sample numbers in the group (unweighted), in the second column, the percentage deviation of the group from the overall mean proportion of inactive households, and in the third column the percentage deviation after controlling for the effects of the other factors.[12] The global proportions inactive for these unweighted data are 4.7 per cent in 1979 and 12.1 per cent in 1986.

Effect of characteristics other than region

For 1979 there are significant effects associated with age, educational qualifications, ethnicity, tenure and the number of children in the household. The unadjusted effects suggest a higher level of inactivity amongst the youngest and oldest ranges of age of household head, substantially higher inactivity amongst those with no qualifications, amongst households of West Indian (though not Asian) origin, and amongst families with large numbers of children. However the most significant effect is associated with tenure, with both local authority and housing association tenants experiencing around twice the level of inactivity of the population as a whole. When the effects of other factors are controlled, the qualification, ethnicity and tenure effects are generally somewhat weaker, though they have the same form. The age effects become somewhat stronger, and the effects of number of children are more clearly linearly increasing.

For 1986, the effect of all covariates is greater than for 1979. This is not simply that the increase in the total size of the inactive population leads to absolute increases in deviations; beyond this, there are relative increases in most factors, and the overall level of variance explained by the grouping increases. With the observed increase in the overall mean number of inactive households by a factor of around 2.5, the absolute values of the deviations should increase by the same level if their significance remained constant. Comparison of the two tables suggests that the age effects have become more pronounced at younger age ranges, that qualification effects have become relatively somewhat weaker, while the effects of numbers of children have remained relatively at about the same level.

17

The position of households of West Indian origin has also remained relatively at about the same level, though of course in absolute terms it has deteriorated; the position of households of South Asian origin has deteriorated substantially in absolute and relative terms. It should be noted that while ethnic minorities have above average chances of being in inactive households, their relatively small numbers mean that they do not form a particularly large proportion of all inactive households. The tenure effects, which were already strongest in 1979 have become even stronger in relative and absolute terms. Even after controlling for other factors, the percentage of inactive council tenant households was 15 per cent above average.

Effect of region

Turning to spatial effects, it is clear that there are substantial differences between regions, and with certain exceptions they are similar in 1979 compared with 1986. Considering unadjusted deviations, areas with above average inactive populations were mainly the conurbations and two peripheral regions of long-term economic decline, Wales and Northern Ireland. The only conurbation areas which did not fall into this category were Greater Manchester and Outer London. How far can one deduce from this that economic inactivity of the sort defined here is particularly concentrated in inner city areas, or indeed is an inner city problem? The first point is that with this data we cannot define narrow inner city areas. All the conurbation areas as defined here include substantial areas which could not be classified as inner city, in either a geographical or social sense. Even then a majority of the inactive households are located outside the conurbations. The regions with an above average share contain 30 per cent of all working age households and 44 per cent of inactive households, hardly an overwhelming level of concentration. The case of Inner London is particularly interesting, given that it is the most closely bounded 'inner' area, and contains large areas which are highlighted in most analyses of multiple deprivation. Its unadjusted share of inactive households was almost 4 per cent above the average, but after controlling for other factors its share is below average. This is mainly because its above average share is 'explained' by its proportion of local authority housing. Now, it might be argued that the share of council housing is itself spatially concentrated in the large cities, so that the tenure effect is in fact a large city effect.[13] However a separate logit analysis found that relative inactivity rates of council tenants were not significantly higher in conurbations than in non-conurbation areas. Inner city underclass hypotheses based on the idea of spatial concentration of problems, would suggest by contrast that there was a process of cumulative causation, so that deprived areas should experience higher levels of inactivity than individual contributing factors alone would explain. The spatial distribution of adjusted deviations shown in Tables 2.8 and 2.9 is intuitively more readily explained by the patterns of long-term economic decline which the large cities and certain regions have experienced. For example, the two areas which showed relatively the greatest deterioration between 1979 and 1986 were South Yorkshire and the West Midlands conurbation: both areas which experienced an exceptionally rapid decline in their industrial base in the early 1980s, compared to their performance in the 1970s.

Conclusion

The analysis in this paper might suggest, at first sight, that Britain had an underclass which represented around 5 per cent of the working age population in 1979, and that in the next seven years it more than doubled, so as to account for around 10 per cent of the population.

One problem which needs to be addressed is the value of defining this group as an underclass. This conclusion focuses attention again on a number of points which are relevant to this.

The first point, stressed in the introduction, is that measures of the potential underclass are highly sensitive to national economic conditions. All the groups identified in this paper have expanded very rapidly in a period of rising national unemployment. In the absence of micro-data sets for the end of the 1980s it is impossible as yet to examine the effects of declining unemployment, but it is clear from published data that at the individual level the numbers of both long-term unemployed and discouraged workers have declined (*Employment Gazette*, April 1990). Presumably they will rise again as the current recession deepens.

The problem is that even when we are speaking of long-term unemployment we do not have evidence that this is really persistent over an entire non-working life. For the vast majority of the long-term unemployed in the mid-1980s unemployment came as a major interruption to a working life and was not a normal condition. They were not so much stable members of an underclass as unstable members of the working class.

However the pattern of labour market experience such as that of the 1980s itself contributes to an instability of future prospects. The experience of unemployment does reduce the prospects of obtaining jobs in the future, and in particular the chances of obtaining stable employment. This is a consequence of both a decline in currently relevant skills and also employer selection strategies. A particularly valuable piece of research bearing on this question would be on whether those who become long term unemployed or inactive in the next years are the same as those who experienced these states in the 1980s. For this we will need life history data.

There are other long term consequences of current labour market inactivity which will have particular impacts for the future of social policy. In particular, members of inactive households, even if they return to paid employment, are likely to have reduced pension entitlements, and their other savings will be depleted. They are thus likely to experience particular problems of poverty in old age.

A relevant issue not addressed in this chapter is the segmentation of the labour market between relatively secure and relatively insecure jobs. The growth of the latter sector has been related to employers' desire to have greater flexibility in their labour input, though inter-sectoral change has also been partly responsible, given the growth of more competitive parts of the service sector. There is evidence that having worked in an industrial sector characterised by higher job turnover is strongly related to individual prospects of unemployment.[14] There seems to be evidence that a record of intermittent unemployment may be converted into long-term unemployment in more unfavourable employment conditions. Thus these changes in the structure of the British labour market may also be contributing to the growth of labour market inactivity.

The analysis of how household inactivity relates to other factors suggest, not unexpectedly, some concentration by social factors, such as housing tenure, age, ethnic origin, possession of educational qualifications and numbers of children. It should be noted that the same factors contribute in broadly similar ways to short-term unemployment. The levels of concentration are not so large as to suggest a social segregation of the inactive population. Neither does the analysis of the spatial distribution suggest a high level of spatial segregation. Quite possibly at a more refined spatial scale higher concentrations might be found, and perhaps situations in which there appear to be processes of cumulative causation occur.

However the implications of focusing only on an urban underclass would be to an identify a very much smaller underclass with additional defining characteristics beyond those used in this analysis. This takes us back to the question of the definition of a possible underclass and its underlying rationale. For example, how far does the existence of families chronically short of work constitute a single policy problem, or is it more useful to consider it as identifying a set of separate problems, whose conjunction has no particular rationale?

Notes

1. N. Buck, 'Social Polarisation in the Inner City: An Analysis of the Impact of Labour Market and Household Change', in M. Cross and G. Payne (eds.), *Social Inequality and the Enterprise Culture* (Falmer, 1991).
2. R. Dahrendorf, 'The Erosion of Citizenship and its Consequences for Us All', *New Statesman*, 12 June 1987; C. Murray, *The Emerging Underclass* (London, Institute for Economic Affairs, 1990).
3. W.G. Runciman, 'How Many Classes are There in Contemporary British Society?', *Sociology*, 24.3 (1990).
4. G. Stedman Jones, *Outcast London* (Oxford, 1971).
5. D.T. Ellwood, 'The Origins of "Dependency": Choices, Confidence, or Culture?', *Focus* 12:1, pp.6-14 University of Wisconsin-Madison, Institute for Research on Poverty (1989).
6. There have been apparent changes in the definition of the household used in the two surveys, the effect of which is that more groups of unrelated adults are likely to be classified together as single households, rather than as a collection of single-person households in 1986 compared to 1979.
7. J. Pahl, *Money and Marriage* (London, 1989).
8. This table and those that follow use LFS weights to gross the sample estimates up to national population estimates.
9. Non-married cohabiting couples are treated in the same way as married couples in this analysis.
10. R.E. Pahl, 'Some Remarks on Informal Work, Social Polarisation and the Social Structure', *International Journal of Urban and Regional Research*, 12 (1988).
11. In Chapter 3, Anthony Heath produces substantially lower estimates of the size of the underclass on the basis of the 1989 British Social Attitudes Survey (4.9% of respondents under 60) and the 1987 British Election Study (6.2%). Although our definitions are marginally different, it is unlikely that the definition used in the present analysis is more extensive. It is likely that there would have been a significant decline between 1986 and 1989, but it is implausible that the proportion could have halved. The other major source of differences are in the sampling frame and the response rates. The 1986 LFS used the postcode address file as a frame, and thus avoids some of the problems of non-registration to which Anthony Heath refers. This response rate was also around 10 per cent higher than that achieved in the other surveys. The differences suggest that these sample factors do indeed differentially affect potential underclass members, and may also suggest that the estimates from the present analysis may still be under-estimates.
12. All main effects were significant at the 0.5% confidence level, and the overall F was 63.9 in 1979 and 177.2 in 1986, with 44 degrees of freedom.
13. This is not an inner city effect, since many of the most deprived council estates, at least outside London, tend to be in outer areas of the conurbations.

14. N. Buck and I.R. Gordon, 'The Beneficiaries of Employment Groups: An Analysis of the Experience of Disadvantaged Groups in Expanding Labour Markets', in V. Hausner (ed.) *Critical Issues in Urban Economic Development*, Vol.2, (Oxford, 1987).

Table 2.1   Distribution of Working Age Households by type

Column percentages

	1979 Household	1986 Household	1986 Family unit
Single person	14.8	14.3	23.3
Couple without children	23.5	23.3	22.0
Couple with children under 16 only	32.7	27.7	26.1
Couple with children both under and over 16	9.1	7.7	7.2
Couple with children over 16 only	10.6	13.0	12.0
Lone parent with children under 16 only	3.5	4.0	4.4
Lone parent with children both under and over 16	1.5	1.3	1.3
Lone parent with children over 16 only	2.5	3.5	3.6
Other households	1.8	5.2	n.a.

Source: Labour Force Surveys, 1979 and 1986

Table 2.2   Work situation of household 'head' by household type: 1979

Row percentages

	Employed	Unemployed less than one year	Other not working
Single person	65.9	3.5	30.6
Couple without children	88.4	1.8	9.8
Couple with children under 16 only	94.1	2.7	3.2
Couple with children both under and over 16	1.8	2.3	5.9
Couple with children over 16 only	92.0	1.4	6.6
Lone parent with children under 16 only	48.7	6.3	45.0
Lone parent with children both under and over 16	57.8	4.3	37.9
Lone parent with children over 16 only	61.2	2.7	36.1
Other households	76.4	4.1	19.5
All households	84.9	2.6	12.5

Source: Labour Force Surveys, 1979 and 1986

Table 2.3   Percentage of households with inactive and long term unemployed 'head' 1979-1986

	1979	1986 (household)	Percentage change 1979-1986	1986 (family unit)
Single person	30.6	37.2	+6.6	32.4
Couple without children	9.8	18.3	+8.6	19.0
Couple with children under 16 only	3.2	9.5	+6.3	10.4
Couple with children both under and over 16	5.9	12.6	+6.7	14.1
Couple with children over 16 only	6.6	14.8	+8.2	15.1
Lone parent with children under 16 only	45.0	54.2	+9.2	53.2
Lone parent with children both under and over 16	37.9	45.1	+7.2	43.9
Lone parent with children over 16 only	36.1	41.7	+5.6	39.2
Other households	19.5	21.6	+2.1	n.a.
All households	12.5	20.5	+8.0	21.7

Source: Labour Force Surveys, 1979 and 1986

Table 2.4   Couple households: work situation of husband by work situation of wife

Row percentages

| | Wife | | |
	Employed	Unemployed Less than one year	Other not working
Husband			
Employed			
1979	56.5	2.9	40.6
1986	63.3	3.7	33.0
Unemployed less than one year			
1979	33.0	7.0	60.0
1986	34.9	10.0	55.2
Other not working			
1979	28.5	1.0	70.5
1986	24.5	2.5	73.1
All couple households			
1979	54.3	2.9	42.7
1986	57.1	3.7	39.2

Source: Labour Force Surveys, 1979 and 1986

Table 2.5   Estimated numbers of inactive and long term unemployed households

	Thousands of households 1979	1986 (household)	Per cent change 1979-1986	Thousands of family units 1986
Single person	701.2	834.5	+19.0	1294.4
Couple				
'household head' basis	704.7	1544.7	+119.2	1672.4
'joint activity' basis	496.8	1124.2	+126.3	1191.7
Lone-parent family	466.6	659.3	+41.3	740.9
Other	55.3	174.6	+215.7	n.a.
Total				
'household head' basis	1927.8	3213.1	+66.7	3707.7
'joint activity' basis	1719.9	2792.6	+62.4	3227.0

Source: Labour Force Surveys, 1979 and 1986

Table 2.6   Estimated numbers of inactive and long-term unemployed households excluding retired, long-term sick and students

	Thousands of households		Per cent change 1979-1986	Thousands of family units 1986
	1979	1986 (household)		
Single person	142.5	393.8	+176.3	582.6
Couple				
'household head' basis	178.5	807.0	+352.1	897.1
'joint activity' basis	139.6	625.9	+348.3	667.1
Lone-parent family	384.2	533.2	+38.8	606.4
Other	16.2	82.1	+406.8	n.a.
Total				
'household head' basis	721.4	1816.1	+151.7	2086.1
'joint activity' basis	682.5	1635.0	+139.6	1856.1

Source: Labour Force Surveys, 1979 and 1986

Table 2.7   Detailed activity description of inactive household 'heads'

	1979 Thousands	1986 Thousands	Per cent change 1979-1986
Long-term unemployed	161.5	578.6	+258.2
Looking after family			
Would like to work	186.2	196.5	+5.5
Does not want work	268.8	261.8	-2.6
Other inactive			
All	65.2	587.4	+809.2
Would like work		307.3	
Does not want work		280.1	
Looking after family and other inactive	520.2	1045.7	+101.0
Total	681.7	1624.3	+138.3

Source: Labour Force Surveys, 1979 and 1986

Table 2.8   Analysis of variance in household inactivity, 1979

Variable & category	N	Unadjusted Dev'n	Eta	Adjusted for independents Dev'n	Beta
Region and conurbation			.07		.05
1 TYNE AND WEAR	1326	2.34		1.60	
2 REST OF NORTH REGION	2315	1.98		1.87	
3 SOUTH YORKSHIRE	1409	-.63		-1.31	
4 WEST YORKSHIRE	2478	-.39		-.21	
5 REST OF YORKS & H'SIDE	1850	.73		.75	
6 EAST MIDLANDS	4031	-.90		-.70	
7 EAST ANGLIA	1923	-.82		-.61	
8 INNER LONDON	2624	1.16		.33	
9 OUTER LONDON	4477	-1.03		-.22	
10 REST OF SE ENGLAND	10683	-1.38		-.67	
11 SOUTH WEST	4813	-.12		.44	
12 WEST MIDLANDS MET.	3167	-.06		-.52	
13 REST OF WEST MID.	2916	-1.52		-1.37	
14 GREATER MANCHESTER	3027	-.05		-.03	
15 MERSEYSIDE	1612	3.83		3.78	
16 REST OF NORTH WEST	2619	-1.16		-.29	
17 WALES	3081	1.27		1.35	
18 CENTRAL CLYDESIDE	1833	2.42		.79	
19 REST OF SCOTLAND	3584	-.43		-1.41	
20 NORTHERN IRELAND	2717	3.57		1.30	
Age			.04		.06
1 16-19	431	2.52		3.94	
2 20-24	3879	1.23		2.22	
3 25-29	6829	.03		.77	
4 30-34	9847	-.73		-.72	
5 35-39	5776	-.95		-1.57	
6 40-44	6774	-.70		-1.33	
7 45-49	7067	-.61		-.95	
8 50-54	7228	.00		-.43	
9 55-59	7811	1.17		.55	
10 60-64	6843	.95		2.21	
Educational qualifications			.12		.09
1 HAS QUALS.	29368	-2.59		-1.54	
2 NO QUALS.	24802	2.98		2.32	
3 DK	8315	.27		-1.47	

Ethnic origin			.04		.02
1	WHITE	57274	-.23		-.09
2	WEST INDIAN/GUYANESE	540	5.14		3.11
3	SOUTH ASIAN	884	.08		.40
4	OTHER / NOT STATED	3787	2.72		.83

Tenure			.16		.13
1	OWNED WITH MORTGAGE	25310	-3.40		-2.84
2	OWNED OUTRIGHT	9443	.50		.87
3	LOCAL AUTHORITY	17611	4.43		3.54
4	HOUSING ASSOCIATION	1888	5.02		2.96
7	PRIVATE RENTED	7869	-.71		-.49

Number of children <16		.06		.08
0	32882	-.76		-1.35
1	11617	.46		.84
2	12271	-.20		1.06
3 or more	5715	3.85		3.76

Multiple R Squared .040
Multiple R .201

Table 2.9   Analysis of variance in household inactivity, 1986

Variable & category	N	Unadjusted Dev'n	Eta	Adjusted for independents Dev'n	Beta
Region and conurbation			.13		.08
1 TYNE AND WEAR	942	8.38		4.64	
2 REST OF NORTH REGION	1672	.10		.34	
3 SOUTH YORKSHIRE	1077	6.65		5.19	
4 WEST YORKSHIRE	1672	1.59		1.43	
5 REST OF YORKS & H'SIDE	1237	-1.35		-.32	
6 EAST MIDLANDS REGION	3166	-.61		.46	
7 EAST ANGLIA REGION	1698	-4.09		-2.81	
8 INNER LONDON	1716	3.86		-.74	
9 OUTER LONDON	3124	-3.81		-1.81	
10 REST OF SE ENGLAND	8276	-5.03		-2.28	
11 SOUTH WEST	3325	-3.08		-.55	
12 WEST MIDLANDS MET.	2055	4.78		3.55	
13 REST OF WEST MID.	2109	-.39		-.04	
14 GREATER MANCHESTER	1991	-.05		-.47	
15 MERSEYSIDE	1130	10.55		8.85	
16 REST OF NORTH WEST	1841	-.53		1.10	
17 WALES	2219	2.23		2.04	
18 CENTRAL CLYDESIDE	1305	6.44		-.24	
19 REST OF SCOTLAND	2717	-.07		-4.36	
20 NORTHERN IRELAND	3095	5.44		2.52	
Age			.12		.10
1 16-19	255	30.25		25.37	
2 20-24	2745	8.26		8.28	
3 25-29	5161	1.27		3.09	
4 30-34	5636	-1.81		-.61	
5 35-39	6625	-2.55		-1.56	
6 40-44	5527	-3.42		-2.61	
7 45-49	5014	-2.71		-1.92	
8 50-54	4760	-1.89		-1.93	
9 55-59	5151	2.13		.74	
10 60-64	5493	3.77		-.35	
Educational qualifications			.18		.09
1 HAS QUALS.	24175	-5.61		-2.89	
2 NO QUALS.	19762	6.14		3.09	
3 DK	2430	5.66		3.64	

Ethnic origin .06 .03
1	WHITE	41040	-.66		-.08
2	WEST INDIAN/GUYANESE	468	12.68		5.54
3	SOUTH ASIAN	791	5.72		5.47
4	OTHER / NOT STATED	4068	4.07		-.91

Tenure .33 .28
1	OWNED WITH MORTGAGE	22712	-8.90		-7.85
2	OWNED OUTRIGHT	7454	-.16		.80
3	LOCAL AUTHORITY	11388	17.21		14.71
4	HOUSING ASSOCIATION	742	12.69		10.61
7	PRIVATE RENTED	3843	-.63		-.91

Number of children <16 .08 .09
0	27088	-1.34		-2.11
1	8229	1.74		2.24
2	7896	-.77		1.78
3 or more	3154	8.92		7.82

Multiple R Squared	.136
Multiple R	.368

3   The Attitudes of the Underclass*

Anthony Heath

This chapter is concerned with the culture of the underclass – their orientations to work and to the family and towards participation in the mainstream economic and political processes of society. Following David Smith's conceptual analysis the underclass is defined as consisting of family units which are economically dependent on state benefits (excluding state pensioners). Whether this group of people constitutes a distinct class in the sense of having distinct long-run interests and constituting a distinct social formation, remains an open question. To resolve that question we need evidence on people's life-histories and social relationships, evidence which is not yet available. But what this chapter explores is whether this group has distinct orientations, in particular whether it exhibits a distinct 'culture of dependency'.[1]

The main data sources that will be used are the 1987 British Election Survey and the 1989 British Social Attitudes Survey.‡ These are nationally representative probability samples (the BES being a sample of the registered electorate and the BSA being a sample of adults aged 18 or over living in private households in Britain). Their sample sizes were 3,826 and 3,029 respectively. These are among the most authoritative surveys covering the social and political attitudes and orientations of Britain's adult population.

There are, however, three important limitations which we must note – the first two of which will affect virtually all survey-based work on the underclass. The first limitation relates to the *scope* of the surveys: the BES is a survey of registered electors; the BSA is a survey of people resident in private households whose addresses were listed in the electoral registers. Some members of the underclass, therefore, will certainly fall outside the scope of these surveys.

---

*   I am grateful to David Smith and Professor Halsey for their suggestions for this chapter and to the participants at the PSI conference for their constructive comments.

‡   The 1989 BSA was directed by Roger Jowell, Sharon Witherspoon and Lindsay Brook of Social and Community Planning Research and was funded by the Sainsbury Family Charitable Trusts. The 1987 BES was directed by Roger Jowell, John Curtice, Julia Field, Sharon Witherspoon and Anthony Heath and was funded by Pergamon press, the Sainsbury Family Charitable Trusts and by the ESRC. I gratefully acknowledge their support. For technical details of these surveys see A.F. Heath et al. *Understanding Political Change: The British Voter 1964-1987* (Oxford, 1991) and R. Jowell, S. Witherspoon and L. Brook, *British Social Attitudes: the 7th Report* (Aldershot, 1990).

The second limitation derives from *response bias*: the response rate to the BES was 70 per cent and that to the BSA was 69 per cent. There is clear evidence that non-respondents differ systematically from respondents,[2] and members of the underclass may be disproportionately likely not to respond.

For both these reasons the surveys are likely to underestimate the size of the underclass, and those members of the underclass who did respond may differ from the non-respondents in their attitudes and orientations.

The third limitation is more specific to our two surveys. Since the surveys are national samples of 3-4,000 respondents, and since the underclass is only a small proportion of the population, the numbers of underclass members in our samples are very small. This means that differences need to be substantively large ones for them to be statistically significant. But since the theories of the underclass postulate substantively large effects, this need not worry us quite so much as the first two limitations. (Note that all differences reported in this paper are statistically significant unless otherwise indicated.)

Before reporting the attitudes and orientations of the respondents, we first describe our operational definition of the underclass and then consider the demographic characteristics of the group thus defined. This will enable us to check whether we have in fact identified the group that most researchers on the underclass have in mind.

The measurement of the underclass

The BSA asks respondents for their (and their partner's) economic status and also asks whether the family unit has received income support (supplementary benefit) within the last five years. Our operational definition of the underclass in the BSA is therefore of family units where neither partner (if there is more than one partner) is currently in paid employment[3] and where a member has been in receipt of income support (supplementary benefit) within the last five years. Excluding respondents of retirement age (taken to be 60 years and over), there were 107 respondents in the survey who met this definition (4.9 percent of the sample aged under 60).

We compare the underclass thus defined with people (aged under 60) who were either in paid employment themselves or had a spouse in paid employment (1,953 respondents). (There was a further small group of 113 respondents who did not fall into either of these categories – largely people dependent on other benefits such as sickness and disability benefits).

Ideally, we would restrict our definition of the underclass further to exclude family units which had had recent experience of paid employment. This cannot be done very readily with the BSA (and for reasons that will become apparent this would reduce the effective size of the sample too much). However, we can distinguish the long-term underclass in the British Election Survey.

In the British Election Survey respondents were asked what was the main source of income for their family unit. They were also asked how long ago it was that they and/or their partner held a paid job (if they were currently without a paid job). From this information we can identify a long-term underclass of family units where the main source of income was income support (supplementary benefit) and where neither partner had been in paid employment for at least five years. There were 71 respondents in this category (2.8 per cent of the total sample aged under 60).

We can also distinguish a category of the short-term underclass, consisting of family units where the main source of income was income support but where one or other partner had been in paid employment within five years. There were 87 respondents in this category

33

(3.4 per cent of the sample). Together, these two categories closely correspond to the definition of the underclass used for the BSA.

The demographic characteristics of the underclass

Tables 3.1a and 3.1b show the age, sex and ethnicity of the underclass according to the BES and BSA data. Our two sources give comfortingly similar results.

The difference between the underclass and the employed families in ethnicity is statistically significant but the great majority of the underclass are clearly white. We certainly should not equate the underclass with membership of minority ethnic groups.

There are also statistically significant differences with respect to age and sex. Members of the long-term underclass are more likely to be female and members of the short-term underclass to be somewhat younger.

Tables 3.2a and 3.2b show that there are also significant differences in the composition of the family units. Members of the underclass are more likely to be single parents with one or more dependent children. This is even more marked in the case of the long-term underclass, although it would be quite wrong to suppose that the typical member of the long-term underclass is a single parent. 38 per cent are, but this is still well short even of a majority.

Tables 3.3a and 3.3b show that members of the underclass are less likely to have qualifications and that their last job is more likely to have been in semi- or unskilled manual work. They are highly likely to live in rented accommodation and to be poor. In all these respects there are more or less substantial differences between the short and long-term underclass, with the latter being considerably more disadvantaged.

In the case of the BES we also have data on the ecology of the underclass. We know the kinds of neighbourhood in which the respondents live.[4] The individuals in the BES have been linked, through their postcodes, with Census data on their enumeration district. The Super Profiles classification of enumeration districts has then been used to group neighbourhoods into various types. Here we distinguish two categories of poor neighbourhood and contrast them with all other neighbourhoods.[5]

The upper panel of Table 3.4 shows that members of the underclass are indeed much more likely to be resident in poor neighbourhoods than are the employed family units. A third of the underclass live in the poorest neighbourhoods, compared with 7 per cent of the employed families. This is scarcely surprising, given the demographic information we have already reported.

Perhaps more interestingly, the lower panel of Table 3.4 shows the composition of the different neighbourhoods. It shows that the underclass make up only one quarter of the residents even in the poorest neighbourhoods. In other words, even these poorest neighbourhoods are ones where employed family units make up the great majority of residents. From the purely ecological point of view, therefore, we have to reject the hypothesis that the underclass constitute a distinct community. This has implications for the distinctiveness of the culture of the underclass. If members of the underclass regularly associate with neighbours who are members of employed family units, then we might expect them to share the attitudes and values of people in employment. A distinct culture is most likely where there is a distinct community, and our ecological data calls into question the idea that the underclass forms a distinct community.[6]

These tables do nonetheless confirm that the underclass which we have been able to distinguish conforms reasonably well to expectations. Members of the underclass are poor, lack educational qualifications, live in rented accommodation, and are less likely to correspond to the nuclear family ideal.

There are of course different possible explanations for these findings. On the one hand, it is quite likely that lack of educational or marketable skills will lead to poor jobs (or none at all), to low income, and to rented housing. Single parents without skills will be particularly vulnerable. On the other hand it could be argued that it is people's attitudes and orientations which cause their lack of qualifications and which lead them to become single parents. Life history data (for example the National Child Development Study) are needed to explore these causal questions.[7] We cannot tackle them here, but we can report on the *current* attitudes and orientations of our samples (recognizing that these may be consequences, rather than causes, of their current situation of dependency). We shall look in turn at orientations towards the family, orientations to work, and political participation.

Orientations to the family

Orientations towards the family are of particular interest. Some views of the underclass hold that it exhibits a breakdown of family life and an irresponsible attitude towards children. The 1989 British Social Attitudes survey asked two batteries of questions relevant to this, although unfortunately these questions were asked only in the self-completion supplement and for half the sample. This reduces our numbers to the lower limits of usefulness (although as we shall see they are still large enough to display some statistically significant differences).

Tables 3.5 and 3.6 report the results. As we can see, the attitudes of the underclass and of mainstream society towards children are very similar. There is just one statistically significant difference, and it is one where the members of the underclass are more likely to give pro-children answers: 93 per cent of the underclass, compared with 79 per cent of members of employed family units, agreed that 'watching children grow up is life's greatest joy'.

There are rather more differences between the underclass and mainstream society in attitudes towards marriage. Perhaps not surprisingly, members of the underclass are more aware of the financial security that marriage brings. They are also less inclined to suppose that people who want children should get married, or that single parents are less able to bring up their children.

Given the relatively large proportion of single parents in the underclass, it is not surprising that they are likely to have more positive attitudes towards single parenthood. We should note, however, that, even when we control for family situation, there are still statistically significant differences between members of the underclass and of the employed family units in their attitudes towards these questions.[8]

Orientations towards work

Orientations towards work are perhaps the crucial area for assessing the notion of a culture of dependency. In the BSA respondents were asked whether they would like to have a paid job now, what were their main reasons for not having a paid job, and what were the characteristics that they think to be important in a job. Tables 3.7, 3.8 and 3.9 give the results.

Table 3.7 compares the members of the underclass with the members of employed family units who were not currently in paid employment themselves. (In other words, the latter group had a partner in paid employment but were themselves unemployed or looking after the home.) There is a highly significant difference between the two groups (p .001),

35

but it is in the opposite direction from that predicted by the culture of dependency thesis. It is the members of the underclass who are much more likely to want a paid job. The notion of a culture of dependency is perhaps better employed elsewhere than in the underclass!

Table 3.8 does not show quite such marked differences, but they are in the same direction.[9] Note that the question which we report here on reasons for not having a paid job outside the home is a multiple response question, and the percentages do not therefore sum to 100.

As we can see, members of the employed family units were more likely to give 'cultural' reasons for not working - in particular saying that they preferred to look after the home. Members of the underclass on the other hand were more likely to give financial reasons – child care costs and the poverty trap – or practical reasons – pregnancy, ill health and a dependent relative.

Finally, Table 3.9 looks at the characteristics which the two groups find important in a job. (Note that in this table we include the employed members of the employed family units.) As with attitudes towards children, the underclass are very similar to the employed family units. There is only one significant difference: members of the underclass seem to be less fussy about their jobs and are less likely to regard independence at work as important. (They are also less likely to want a lot of leisure time, but this difference does not quite reach statistical significance.)

Overall, then, these results give no support to the notion of a culture of dependency among the underclass. While our sample is very small, we have seen that it is not so small as to preclude statistically significant differences, but all the differences are in the 'wrong' direction.

Orientations towards politics

Theories of the underclass emphasise that the members of the underclass are not integrated into mainstream society and do not participate in the conventional institutions of the society. This is of course true by definition in the case of work but is an empirical matter in the case of politics.

Most people's participation in politics is limited largely to voting. Few people participate more actively (in pressure groups, political parties and political protests).[10] The 1987 British Election Survey is a particularly valuable one in that it has been linked with the official records of people's turnout at the general election.[11] (The party for which people voted is of course secret, but official records are kept of whether registered electors voted or not, and these records are available for public inspection at the Lord Chancellor's Office. For further details see Swaddle and Heath 1989.) This information is particularly valuable for us as it means that we have valid behavioural data on the underclass as well as their own reports. As Lewis pointed out 'People with a culture of poverty are aware of middle-class values; they talk about them and even claim some of them as their own, but on the whole they do not live by them. Thus, it is important to distinguish between what they say and what they do'.[12] By examining the official data on turnout, we can see what they actually do.

Table 3.10 shows that there was indeed a statistically significant difference between the actual turnout of members of the long-term underclass and that of members of employed family units. All the same, turnout was still quite high at 68 per cent even among members of the long-term underclass, so once again it would be quite wrong to typify the underclass as non-participants in the political process. (Because of non-response bias, the values for all three categories in Table 10 will *overestimate* the turnout of the populations sampled, although we should also note that the official figure for overall turnout in 1987 – 75 per cent – is almost certainly an *underestimate* because of errors, redundancy and ageing of the electoral register.)

We also have some measures in the BES of respondents' feelings of political efficacy and their orientations towards the political system. These are shown in Table 3.11 and confirm and develop the results on turnout. They show that members of the underclass have a significantly lower sense of efficacy and a greater feeling of cynicism about the political system.

Education is one of the major determinants of political efficacy, and, as we saw earlier, members of the underclass have markedly lower educational qualifications than other people do. Once we control for education, we find that the differences in turnout and in sense of political efficacy are no longer statistically significant. What we see in Tables 3.10 and 3.11, therefore, should perhaps be regarded as an effect of education, not an effect of underclass membership.[13]

Conclusions

The limitations of the BSA and BES samples must be borne in mind. The limitations of scope and non-response bias mean that we should be wary of asserting that the underclass possesses certain characteristics. It may be that the non-respondent members of the underclass do differ from mainstream society in the ways predicted by the theorists. All we can say with confidence is that the data available to us fail to confirm the notion of a culture of dependency. We can also hazard the guess that the actual proportion of non-respondent members of the underclass is no more than 1 or 2 per cent of the population. So if there is a hidden underclass with a culture of dependency it is likely to be quite a small-scale phenomenon.

A second important point to which our results draw attention is the danger of drawing causal conclusions from descriptive findings. Members of the underclass do indeed seem to differ from mainstream society in their political participation, their sense of efficacy and cynicism. But there are no good grounds for thinking that they differ because of a distinct culture associated with the underclass. The members of the underclass simply illustrate tendencies that are widespread in mainstream society as well. Thus among the employed population political participation varies by educational level, and it is the low educational level of members of the underclass that accounts for their low participation.

A third important point is the heterogeneity of the underclass, both in the kinds of people that fall into it and in their attitudes and orientations. We must beware of drawing *typifications* where there are merely *differences*. Members of the underclass do indeed exhibit lower political participation, but nonetheless the majority of those in our survey did turn out to vote at the last general election. It would therefore be quite wrong to talk of a culture of non-participation. This is perhaps the most important lesson of this research.

Notes

1. The classic statement on this theme is by O. Lewis, 'The Culture of Poverty', in D.P. Moynihan (ed.) *On Understanding Poverty: Perspectives from the Social Sciences* (New York, 1968); see also C. Murray, *The Emerging Underclass* (London: Institute of Economic Affairs, 1990); and for an early trenchant critique, see C.A. Valentine, *Culture and Poverty: Critique and Counter-Proposals* (Chicago, 1968).
2. See, for example, K. Swaddle and A.F. Heath, 'Official and Reported Turnout in the British General Election of 1987', *British Journal of Political Science* 19 (1989); and

G. Farrant and C. O'Muircheartaigh, 'Components of Non-Response Bias in the British Election Surveys' in A.F. Heath et al., *Understanding Political Change: The British Voter 1964-1987* (Oxford, 1991).

3. Along with paid employment we also include people waiting to take up paid employment, those on job training schemes, and those in full-time education.

4. I am very grateful to Martin Harrop and Stan Openshaw for linking the BES with the neighbourhood data. For further details see M. Harrop, A.F. Heath and S. Openshaw, 'Does Neighbourhood Influence Voting Behaviour - and Why?' in P. Norris (ed.) *British Parties and Elections Yearbook* (London, 1991).

5. Our poorest category of neighbourhood consists of enumeration districts (EDs) characterised by council accommodation and high unemployment rates. The next poorest consists of EDs characterised by council accommodation and blue-collar workers.

6. To determine whether the underclass constitutes a distinct community we really need data on patterns of social association as well as those on place of residence.

7. For a relevant report on the NCDS data, see D. Pilling, *Escape from Disadvantage* (London: The Falmer Press in association with the National Children's Bureau, 1990).

8. In a regression analysis of attitudes to MARVIEW7 ('a single mother can bring up her child as well as a married couple'), membership of the underclass had a significant effect (at the .05 level) after controlling for marital status, presence of dependent children, age, sex, ethnicity, tenure, class of last job, educational qualifications, and income. Age, sex, marital status and tenure also had significant net effects. Similar results were obtained for MARVIEW8 ('a single father can bring up his child as well as a married couple').

9. Note the difference in the Ns for the employed family units in Tables 3.7 and 3.8. Since these questions were asked in the self-completion supplement they depend on the respondents' own definitions of unemployed, looking after the home, and so on. It appears that the larger proportion of the employed family units subscribe to a self-definition of themselves as looking after the home.

10. The 1987 BES does contain information on some of these other political activities but I have not found any statistically significant differences between members of the underclass and mainstream society.

11. I am very grateful to Kevin Swaddle and Debs Ghate for linking the BES data with the official records on turnout.

12. O. Lewis, 'The Culture of Poverty', in D.P. Moynihan (ed.) *On Understanding Poverty: Perspectives from the Social Sciences* (New York, 1968), p.190.

13. In a logistic regression of turnout, membership of the underclass did not have a significant effect after controlling for marital status, presence of dependent children, age, sex, ethnicity, tenure, class of last job, educational qualifications and age. In a regression analysis of efficacy ('people like me have no say in what the government does') membership of the underclass did not have a significant effect, but age, sex, ethnicity, class, income and qualifications did.

Table 3.1a   Composition of the underclass by ethnicity, age, and gender: BSA 1989

Percentages

	Non-white	Aged under 35	Women	N
Underclass	7	54	65	107
Employed family units	3	43	52	1952

Source: 1989 BSA, respondents aged 18-59

Table 3.1b   Composition of the underclass by ethnicity, age, and gender. BES 1987

Percentages

	Non-white	Aged under 35	Women	N
Long-term underclass	6	42	62	71
Short-term underclass	9	58	49	87
Employed family units	4	43	49	2393

Source: 1987 BES, respondents aged 18-59

Table 3.2a Composition of the underclass by family situation: BSA 1989

Row percentages

	Married with no children under 16	Married with children under 16	Single with no children under 16	Single with children under 16	N
Underclass	19	30	23	28	107
Employed family units	35	40	21	4	1952

Source: 1989 BSA, respondents aged 18-59

Table 3.2b Composition of the underclass by family situation: BES 1987

Row percentages

	Married with no children under 16	Married with children under 16	Single with no children under 16	Single with children under 16	N
Long-term underclass	14	20	28	38	71
Short-term underclass	8	40	33	18	87
Employed family units	34	42	23	2	2393

Source: 1987 BES, respondents aged 18-59

Table 3.3a Characteristics of the underclass: BSA 1989

Percentages

	With no quali- fications	With low skilled last job	In rented accomo- dation	With household income below£5,000	N
Underclass	60	52	78	79	94
Employed family units	31	21	21	4	1704

Source: 1989 BSA, respondents aged 18-59. The Ns are for the income data

Table 3.3b Characteristics of the underclass: BES 1987

Percentages

	With no quali- fications	With low skilled last job	In rented accomo- dation	With household income below£5,000	N
Long-term underclass	66	68	85	86	69
Short-term underclass	49	44	70	81	79
Employed family units	30	21	20	6	2109

Source: 1987 BES, respondents aged 18-59. The Ns are for the income data

Table 3.4   Neighbourhood of residence: underclass and employed family units: BES 1987

Row percentages

	poorest neighbourhoods	Living in next poorest	other neighbourhoods		N
Long-term underclass	35	26	39	100%	80
Short-term underclass	33	12	55	100%	89
Employed family units	7	14	79	100%	2056

Column percentages

	poorest neighbourhoods	Living in next poorest	other neighbourhoods
Long-term underclass	12	6	2
Short-term underclass	12	3	2
Employed family units	76	92	96
	100%	100%	100%
N	241	379	2056

Source: 1987 BES, respondents aged 18-59

Table 3.5   Attitudes towards children: BSA 1989

	Underclass	Employed family units	Significance
Per cent taking pro-children stance			
It is better *not* to have children because they are such a heavy burden (% disagreeing)	91	89	NS
Children are more trouble than they are worth (% disagreeing)	85	87	NS
Watching children grow up is life's greatest joy (% agreeing)	93	79	.05
Having children interferes too much with the freedom of parents (% disagreeing)	71	73	NS
A marriage without children is not fully complete (% agreeing)	39	38	NS
People who have never had children lead empty lives (% agreeing)	22	17	NS
N	38	808	

Source: 1989 BSA, self-completion supplement, half sample; respondents aged 18-59

Table 3.6   Attitudes towards marriage: BSA 1989

	Underclass	Employed family units	Significance
Per cent agreeing with each proposition			
People who want children ought to get married	47	64	.05
Married people are generally happier than unmarried people	22	25	NS
The main purpose of marriage ... is to have children	18	15	NS
The main advantage of marriage is ... financial security	31	11	.001
Personal freedom is more important than the companionship of marriage	12	11	NS
It is better to have a bad marriage than no marriage at all	10	2	.001
A single mother can bring up her child as well as a married couple	60	33	.001
A single father can bring up his child as well as a married couple	51	27	.01
Couples don't take marriage seriously enough when divorce is easily available	61	54	NS
Homosexual couples should have the right to marry one another	15	13	NS
N	38	856	

Source: 1989 BSA, self-completion supplement, half sample; respondents aged 18-59

Table 3.7   Proportion who would like to have a paid job now

Row percentages

	Yes full-time	Yes part-time	No	N
Underclass	53	33	14	46
Employed family units	11	46	43	138

Source: 1989 BSA self-completion supplement, half sample; respondents aged 18-59 who did not have a paid job of 10 hours a week (or more)

Table 3.8   Main reasons for not having a paid job outside the home

Percentages

	Underclass	Employed family units
Raising children	59	50
Retired/too old	0	2
Prefer looking after home/family	5	21
No jobs available	5	5
Unsuitable for available jobs	4	2
Feel married women shouldn't work	0	2
Husband against working	0	4
Voluntary worker	0	3
Pregnant/ill health	20	8
Dependent relative	9	2
Poverty trap	14	1
Already works less than 10 hours a week	0	6
Child care costs	11	6
Unpaid work/family business	0	1
N	49	219

Source: 1989 BSA, self-completion supplement, half sample; respondents aged 18-59 who do not have a paid job of 10 hours a week (or more) and who are looking after the home.

Table 3.9   Characteristics found important in a job

Percentages

	Underclass	Employed family units	Significance
Percentage finding each characteristic important			
Job security	94	96	NS
High income	84	83	NS
Good opportunities for advancement	80	84	NS
A job that leaves a lot of leisure time	36	50	NS
An interesting job	97	96	NS
A job that allows someone to work independently	48	67	.01
A job that allows someone to help other people	63	64	NS
A job that is useful to society	68	61	NS
A job with flexible working hours	45	48	NS
N	48	769	

Source: 1989 BSA self-completion supplement, half sample; respondents aged 18-59

Table 3.10   Turnout at the 1987 General Election

Row percentages

	Yes	No	N
Long-term underclass	68	32	68
Short-term underclass	79	21	84
Employed family units	82	18	2325

Sources:1987 BES, respondents aged 18-59; Lord Chancellor's office

Table 3.11 Political efficacy and cynicism

Percentages

	Long-term underclass	Short-term underclass	Employed family units	Significance
Percentage agreeing with the proposition				
People like me have no say in what the government does	68	61	45	.001
Sometimes politics and government seem so complicated that a person like me cannot really understand what is going on	78	73	54	.001
It doesn't really matter which party is in power, in the end things go on much the same	48	59	28	.001
Parties are only interested in people's votes, not in their opinions	73	71	53	.001
N	71	79	2316	

Source: 1987 BES, self-completion supplement

4   Theories and Explanations of the Underclass

David Willetts

Origins of the debate

Today's debate about the British underclass bears a striking resemblance to two other such debates – in 19th century Britain and in America today. The Victorians sharply distinguished between 'poverty' and 'pauperism'. 'Paupers' were, in 19th century terminology, people who were dependent for a long while on poor relief. After we had the rediscovery of poverty in the 1960s and ambitious new welfare programmes launched as a result, it was perhaps inevitable that it would be followed by the rediscovery of pauperism.

We also need to compare very carefully the contemporary British and American analyses of the 'underclass'. In the USA the issue can be traced back to the 'War on Poverty' launched by Presidents Kennedy and Johnson. Their objective was, in Kennedy's words, 'a hand up not a handout'. They were not interested simply in raising the living standards of people who had no income of their own. They were aiming at something much more ambitious (and typically American) – establishing these people on their own feet, making their own way in the world. That is why one of the ways in which Americans measure the failure of the Kennedy programmes is by 'latent poverty'. They do not regard all low incomes as being the same. 'Latent poverty' measures the income which you would have if you were not receiving welfare. Its equivalent in British terminology is 'original income' (incomes before benefit payments). The tables at the back of the British statistics for the original incomes of the poorest 20 per cent and the poorest 40 per cent, show a pattern less dramatic than the American one but along similar lines. Original incomes, have indeed been falling during the 1970s and 1980s. We have reached the stage where the less affluent 50 per cent of the population get nearly 50 per cent of their total incomes from the state.

America did not just experience the failure of the high-spending Kennedy programmes of the 1960s. In the 1970s they tried tax benefit integration and the Nixon Family Assistance Plan. It was a classic American attempt at designing a sparkling new tax benefit system. They would get rid of really high marginal rates of tax and benefit withdrawal by introducing a tapering tax credit instead. There were two enormous Income Maintenance Experiments in Seattle and Denver – SIME and DIME as they are known. Those experiments had depressing results. They found that despite lowering the marginal rate of taxation and benefit withdrawal combined, there was an increase in unemployment amongst the group on the new, more generous tax credit compared with the control group on the old benefit system. They also found, even more disconcertingly, that people who were offered free training places were less likely subsequently to find work than people

48

who were not offered free training. The intuitive explanation of that apparently perverse result was that putting people on a training programme has two conflicting effects. One does indeed increase their skills and their employment potential. But secondly one increases their own judgement of their reserve wage, the wage they ought to be able to command after the training programme. If the training programme is sold too ambitiously (promising it is going to leave beneficiaries with very high skills and a good job) there is a risk that you raise their reserve wage by more than you raise their earnings potential.

America during the 1960s and 1970s fought an ambitious war on poverty which ended up looking more like Vietnam than like Grenada. It did not achieve the objectives which people hoped it would achieve when they first embarked on it. The current, rather fraught but also very stimulating American debate on the long-term causes of poverty derives from the sense that a lot of well-intentioned people for the last 20 years have been trying to design programmes to help people out of poverty and have not been as successful as they hoped.

Now we in the UK are coming to this debate. The term 'underclass' is highly charged politically. Our ministers here do not refer to the underclass. I am not even sure whether prospective parliamentary candidates should refer to the underclass. The underclass could well be a quasi-Marxist concept. So the term is used here provisionally and hypothetically, and enclosed within imaginary quotation marks.

Defining an underclass

Three key groups – the long-term unemployed, unskilled workers in erratic employment, and younger single mothers are all likely to be dependent on Income Support. The simplest definition of the 'underclass' is long-term or frequent claimants of income support. That working definition enables us to avoid some of the more rarefied and arid theoretical disputes. But is there any connection between those different categories of long-term or frequent claimants of income-support? Young single mothers are by definition female. The long-term unemployed are by and large male. How can we link together the disparate members of this group who are long-term benefit claimants?

One of the most interesting authors on this subject is Professor William Julius Wilson of Chicago. He has put forward the interesting concept of the 'marriageable pool'. It is an attempt to tie together unemployment amongst men, the criminal record of some young men and the increase in the number of young single mothers. His argument is that the pool of marriageable men, from which women might be expected to find husbands, is shrinking in major American cities. Even if the women would like to be married to a man with a traditional, wage-earning bread-winning role (without making any assumptions about whether the women themselves might want to work or not), men like that to whom they might get married are in short supply. A lot of the available men are either unemployed, or casually employed, or engaged in crime and in and out of jail. The marriageable pool is shrinking.

Wilson ties this in with an argument about the changing nature of the ghetto. A traditional ghetto, a ghetto in the classic European Jewish sense, is a complete community with community leaders, and a whole set of community roles. Everyone is trapped in it because of systematic discrimination from outside. Americans would say that the Harlem of the inter-War years or the immediate post-War period, had some of those features of a classic ghetto community.

If that discrimination then goes – obviously something which we all agree is a good thing – the shock to the culture of the ghetto is considerable. There are, for the first time, opportunities outside the ghetto. The people who can get out do get out. Professor Wilson argues that this process leaves a rather different sort of ghetto community behind; it is a much more hopeless group without the same community structure. The Harlem of the 1980s is supposed to look and feel very different from the Harlem of the 1950s.

This ties in with a fundamental question in political philosophy, about the relationship between mobility and community. It may be mobility which is creating these communities which are, if you like, more dependent. When people can move around, and live in neighbourhoods with the people they choose then this paradoxically can lead to an underclass problem in which some groups are trapped.

If Britain is becoming a more mobile society it would suggest that this sort of social problem might also increase. This is difficult to measure, but the political scientists offer some evidence: Professor Anthony King has observed for example that there are fewer and fewer marginal seats because we live in more homogeneous communities. Social mobility in Britain means that we are by and large establishing ourselves in communities where we live with people like ourselves. One theoretical question prompted by the underclass debate is therefore the extent to which more mobility and the underclass go together.

Social policy and concepts of citizenship

There is one striking difference in terminology between Britain and America. The Americans distinguish sharply between 'social security' (what we would call contributory benefits) and 'welfare' which we in Britain would regard as non-contributory means tested benefits. The American experts troubled with the 'underclass' are not talking about their 'social security' at all. Charles Murray's book, *Losing Ground*, does not talk about old age pensioners or people claiming contributory unemployment insurance. What he is preoccupied with is Aid to Families with Dependent Children (AFDC), their major means-tested non-contributory benefit which goes largely to single parents. 'Social security' in America is not contentious.

Behind this definitional point is an important philosophical issue. To what extent should we perceive social security (in its British sense, of that is all the benefits which the Department of Social Security distributes) as mutual insurance for all of us against adverse life events? We all pay in and we all expect at various stages of the life cycle to take out again. That's one model of what a social security system is trying to do. There is an alternative model, captured by the American term 'welfare', which sees it as something that *we* give to help *them*. It is money we give to distinct groups of people with distinct difficulties unlikely to be experienced by many of their fellow-citizens. It is the difference between the retirement pension and Income Support. The question is: to what extent is the British social security system not a mutual system in which we chip in and take out, but a system whereby the working population essentially finances special needy groups? There is not necessarily anything wrong with either conception of the role of social security in Britain. But we need to distinguish the different rationales of the two different approaches.

This raises not just theoretical questions, but also empirical questions which we cannot yet answer. To what extent are we all, over our lifetimes, likely to be the victims of unforeseen, and unfortunate life events? There are different views about the prospects of the Essex longitudinal study resolving some of these questions. At the moment nobody knows to what extent we can identify in the UK a distinct group of people who are likely to be the long-term recipients of income support.

As well as longitudinal research we also need more horizontal research. It would be interesting to know whether there are patterns in use of other services of the welfare state, not just benefits. GPs, for example, will say a high proportion of their caseload consists of a relatively small number of people. Although the mean number of visits to a GP in a year is approximately 5.5 per person, the median is a lot lower. To what extent is it the same group of people who are the frequent visitors to GPs, who are also heavy users of social services and are also on income support? We simply do not know.

The debate on behaviour: is economics sovereign?

There is along-standing literature about a so called culture of dependency. The original work by Charles Murray, *Losing Ground*, which was published in 1984 and aroused so much debate in America, was an attempt to apply Occam's razor to this debate on culture. He was not yet another theorist of the culture of dependency. His argument was that you do not need any cultural explanations of why some groups of people are long-term dependent on benefit. All you need is a simple economic model in which you compare what it is that people collect on benefit, compared with the alternative opportunities around them. It was a deliberate attempt to escape from cultural explanations and to move to an account based on economic incentives.

The original Charles Murray economic arguments are not unlike the arguments about short-termism in British industry – people are being offered a rational short-term option which is long-term irrational. Somehow what we are doing as policy makers is leading them up the garden path. We are offering people a sustainable short-term option which is long-term damaging. This is not to say that the aspirations or attitudes of people who are long-term claimants of benefit need be different from the mass of the population. All the American evidence is that in their aspirations people who are on benefits are not significantly different from the rest of us. The question is to what extent they have, or believe they have, the ability to meet those aspirations, and to what extent are they prepared to take the first few steps to fulfil their aspirations.

Charles Murray's arguments have been under a lot of attack in American in the past few years. One of the main lines of criticism has been that the real value of AFDC (basically the only benefit this is all about), fell during the 1970s by up to 25 per cent. Yet it was during the 1970s that the big increase in young single parents occurred. To what extent can Charles Murray consistently maintain an economic incentivist account of what is going on?

The defence of the economic account is that we all have such high expectations of how social security (in the British sense) can help people, and such an enormous amount of money is spent, that it seems unlikely that it simply reflects problems of long-term poverty, long-term dependency on benefit whose origins lie elsewhere. To have a massive public expenditure programme which simply reflected other social changes driven by other public sector programmes – poor quality education and training for example – but was not itself in any way a causal factor, seems to me implausible. When a group of social security experts get together, they say well of course you really have to look at training or education or something else. Every one is always tempted to make someone else's policy area the exogenous variable which explains what's going on, and theirs a mere passive response to the problem which someone else has caused. It just seems implausible that the benefit system has such a weak role in the pattern of causation.

Much of the dependency and underclass debate boils down to a classic moral hazard problem. To what extent, when you alleviate the circumstances of people who have got themselves into a mess, do you increase the chances that more people will get themselves into that mess in future. There's a lot of empirical work to be done on what the trade-off is, but in principle there must be a moral hazard issue here.

A lot of us would probably agree on what an ideal benefit system would be. It would be in practice generous, but believed to be tough. That's the only way round the moral hazard problem. It would be a system in which it was believed that you would have a rough ride, but if you got into a mess and ended up needing help on the other side of what one might call a veil of ignorance, one then discovered, lo and behold, that actually the system was compassionate and sympathetic. The trouble is that maintaining a set of public beliefs about the system which differ from the reality is, to say the least, very difficult. You could argue that the Victorians achieved it but it requires social pressures like hypocrisy and shaming. It is because those pressures are breaking down that this sort of debate has opened up again.

The importance of values

If you are in inner-city Washington or New York the best single predictor of whether you are going to get a job is whether or not you are a regular church-goer. Church-going is the best predictor of the lot, better even than education. What does this tell us about the role of values? As soon as one starts talking about values people get worried. Dependency, or even more, delinquency, are highly charged concepts. But we cannot escape moral judgements. The social security system itself embodies a set of moral views about our obligations to our fellow citizens. The Beveridge Report with its marvellous Bunyanesque prose is an obvious appeal to moral instincts about what we owe our fellow citizens. These moral questions cannot be avoided in any discussion about social security. People who talk about social security as if it is purely a technocratic mater are in danger of undermining the moral and cultural base on which the social security system rests. It rests on a particular set of views that people in this country take about their obligations to their fellow citizens.

There is one particular group of people whose values we need to respect. One might call them (if it is not too crass) the respectable poor. They are the people who are living just above benefit, the people who are making ends meet in low-paid work and not in receipt of income support. What is it that makes the life of a low paid worker valuable and satisfying? This is the sort of question which Charles Murray asks us to address. Part of what makes it satisfying is that at least you are helping to keep your family by your own efforts. Collecting a paypacket and being able to sustain oneself independently is itself a major source of satisfaction to people and it is not one to be ignored.

If you can manage to collect a very similar income in benefits without going through the bore of working five days a week there comes a point when the person who is working thinks he is being made a fool. He wonders to what extent his belief that his work is valuable, because at least it can sustain a family, is being undermined by other people who can make nearly as much money from benefit. One of the interesting aspects of the social security system is what you learn when you talk to the people in the fraud section of a local benefit office. The people in the fraud section do not have a sophisticated intelligence system which enables them to go and track down social security fraud. They rely on tip-offs from members of the public. The letters that they get from the members of the public reveal a very clear moral sense of what it is that the social security system is trying to do and who is entitled to social security and the circumstances in which people should not be claiming social security. It is very dangerous to ignore those values which surround and sustain the social security system.

The problems of state action

The Americans have found that the war on poverty was not quite as easy as a bunch of ambitious social policy planners thought when they worked for Kennedy or Johnson. Now they have gone to the other extreme. Charles Murray, if you take him literally, is proposing an impossibility theorem. He is saying nothing works. Increasing expenditure, community initiatives, workfare – none of them work. That is too pessimistic. I don't believe myself in the impossibility of effective social action. But we have learnt that programmes need to be devised very carefully, and rigorously. Alleviating poverty is a much more complicated business than just paying out social security cheques to people.

The sort of question which one has to confront is to what extent are we entitled to expect certain types of behaviour from people to whom we are giving benefit. In national insurance, the conditionality is clear: you pay in your contributions and you collect money back when the conditions are met. Although the economists have never been able to make sense of national insurance, regarding it as sort of actuarial mumbo jumbo, it is an extremely important part of our political culture. The opinion surveys conducted for Norman Fowler's social security review showed that people are much more prepared to pay national insurance than tax.

The question is whether there is any degree of conditionality at all for people on non-contributory income support. Beveridge himself envisaged that after six months on national assistance recipients of benefits would be expected to go onto some training scheme. Workfare of the tough West Virginian variety is clearly not a viable option – it is not acceptable. But proper testing of being available for work or actively seeking work is feasible.

There is a cycle here in social policy. When unemployment is low or on a downward trend, people are pretty rigorous about testing availability for work. As one moves through the economic cycle and unemployment starts rising then suddenly 500 able-bodied keen men turn up at the benefit office on the Monday morning saying they were sacked on the Friday afternoon. Asking them all whether they're genuinely seeking work or not is a bit of a farce. So those tests of availability are relaxed because there is not much point. What we have actually got in the whole history of recent legislation changing from availability for work to actively seeking work, is a debate on what we should expect of unemployed people on income support which closely follows the economic cycle.

Another problem in devising a sensible benefit system is creaming. And one of the complaints made about classic public sector training programmes is that they focus on the easy cases. If you are running a public sector training scheme and the measure of success set by the Department of Employment is the percentage of people on your training scheme who go on to find jobs, the sort of people you want on your training schemes are the best of the unemployed. You design, intentionally or not, a scheme which enables you to identify the sort of people who will enable you to look like a success. You have an application form. If they can't fill in the application form, then there isn't a place for you on the scheme. That eliminates the estimated 25 per cent of the long-term unemployed who are feared to be nearly illiterate. One of the obvious failures of public policy is to put crude success criteria on people running training schemes, which means that instead of dealing with the unemployed whom no-one else would help they are instead targeting people who might have got some commercially financed training for themselves anyway.

Conclusion

The idea of an 'underclass' is not simple or straightforward. It is controversial both in America and here in Great Britain. But it has driven us to face once more difficult and important questions about the causes of poverty and the true role of social security.

5   Footnotes to the Discussion

Ralf Dahrendorf

I propose to add four footnotes to the discussion. They may, in part, turn out to be land mines but they are certainly not intended to kill.

Nature and significance of the underclass
First, in every age there are those who drop through the net which catches full members of society. I have at home Charles Booth's *Map of London Poverty*; in the 1890s people spoke in much more candid language, so that the map shows ink-coloured blots where people lived who were 'vagrants, drunks, unemployables, criminals', in other words horrible people with whom nobody wanted to live. There were quite a few areas in London at that time which are painted in that particular colour, and if you go 40 years further back and read Mayhew, you get some beautiful stories about the underclass. In other words, there is nothing new about the phenomenon of people who are not a part of life as those who represent the dominant values of a society would like to see it. I agree entirely with David Smith that it would be nice to find a minimal, or even an operational definition. One might try David Willetts's proposal and talk about the long-term claimants of public support or even those who are entitled to public support; something of that kind might be useful. Certainly I believe that it makes sense to talk about people in human societies who are not able, or perhaps willing, or both, to participate fully in the economic, the political and the social life of the communities in which they are living. This means, incidentally, that if there are formal systems of social support, these are not likely to reach them in quite the way in which they are intended to reach them. Moneys are likely to be used for objectives which have little to do with the objectives for which these systems have been created.

The question of whether such groups exist seems to me spurious. I am quite sure that these groups are not classes in any technical sense, a subject to which I shall return. I have no difficulty with the word underclass because I can accommodate my language to everyday language, but there is no technical or proper sociological sense in which this particular category can ever be called a class. Even that is neither here nor there; the interesting questions, as David Smith put it so well, are the empirical questions: is the underclass large or small? I have a hunch that in the 19th century it was very much larger than it is today. Is it growing or shrinking? I was very interested in the empirical papers this morning because they seem to indicate that it may be growing in Britain today. Is it hard or soft? I think this is William Julius Wilson's term. In other words, is the underclass a soft category with permeable boundaries, so that it is easy for some to move out and others to drop back into it; or is it a solid, fixed group of people with their own culture? Does it correlate with other important features of social life or doesn't it? Is there something random about membership of this category or is it systematic? Does race matter or doesn't it matter? In this context, the discussion of the differences between American cities and British cities is quite important; even the race issues presents itself very differently. For example, one of Wilson's important theses is that in some of the black ghettos, what he calls the 'role models' have disappeared, so that while there is a group of successful blacks, those who grow up in Chicago, or in the Bronx, never see any black person who has been successful. Now, that is fortunately not true in Britain; it is still the case that if you grow up as a minority youngster you are able to see members of your minority who have done rather well, so that there is not this total dissociation from the opportunities of a society in which you are living.

However, my first footnote really says that there is a serious issue of the category of those who are excluded, but in Britain things are not quite as bad as they might be, and as they are in other parts of the world. The possibility – or impossibility – of making general statements about the category is itself an interesting fact and if one has to grope for general statements and finds it difficult to discover sensible things to say which are true for a significant number of people, one does not need to worry quite as much as in other parts of the world. I think the American underclass and especially the ghetto underclass problem is one of the most serious problems in the entire civilised world; I am not blaming Americans because they have tried very hard to cope with it, much harder than we have at anything, but it is nevertheless still there.

Why people fall into the underclass

Second footnote: why do people drop through this net which societies have? They do so because for some reason they do not want to or do not find it possible to comply with the dominant values of a society. In my own analysis, there are two sets of values which are particularly relevant in this connection: one of these has to do with work and the other has to do with families. The issue of work has been alluded to a number of times this morning, with rather important statements. One issue that needs to be looked at closely when discussing the category of those who drop out is to what extent a developed modern economy needs everybody who could conceivably be employed, to what extent it could do quite well with two, five, ten, fifteen, twenty per cent unemployment and nevertheless produce satisfactory growth rates. I think this is a very important issue, and one which has a lot to do with the ability of those who have dropped out of the labour market to come back in. Incidentally, even within Europe different countries seem to deal with this issues in rather different ways. Germany has had two million unemployed for quite a long time now, to say nothing of another million who are either conscripts or students, and are, therefore, taken off the labour market. And yet economic development in Germany is very satisfactory. So something is changing about the nature of work, and our values which emphasise work and the need for work do not seem to tally with the economic basis of our society. This is one of the reasons why many people have but a tenuous hold on the labour market.

Similar observations could be made about the family, especially the old ideal of a complete family with two children. Things have changed quite significantly. David Willets has made a dramatic point, the Pat Moynihan point about American blacks. The change in their family structures is quite extraordinary and is one which is very hard to explain, for among them the complete family is almost the total exception, it describes 10-15 per cent of all blacks, not many more. There are other changes, for instance the fact that two incomes are needed to sustain a family nowadays. This too has something to do with poverty and who drops into poverty. Thus dominant values, which still exist somewhere, do not satisfy the needs of all people in our societies and because they do not satisfy these needs some people drop through the net. Not surprisingly, we do not quite know what to do about them as we get these phenomena of persistent unemployment, persistent poverty, poverty of single parent families, and so on.

Not a class but a challenge to dominant values
Third footnote: The key point in theoretical terms about the underclass seems to me to be that it is precisely not a class. Classes are essentially necessary social forces. It is no accident that Marx tried to link classes, not just to relations but to forces of production; he saw classes as being based on certain central social needs, one class which presides over the existing values and laws and rules and mode of production and the other class which represents some new opportunity for the future, some chances of development. The whole point about the underclass or the category of those who have dropped through the net is that they are not needed in this sense. Can I say in parenthesis that the real equivalent of the underclass on an international scale is the very poor countries. Their position in a world society and the extent to which they are needed or not needed presents analogous challenges, as does the extent to which there is an actual interest on the part of the richer countries in doing something for the poor or not. There may not be such an interest; there certainly is no massive and identifiable interest on the part of the official classes of the advanced societies to do something about the underclass. They could live quite happily with an underclass of 5, 10, 12, 15 per cent for a very long time and if they are rich enough and have arrangements like the Federal Republic of Germany, they can feed the underclass and not bother about the fact that they are not a part of the labour market or indeed may not be a part of political or social life in general. At the same time, it seems to me that tolerating a group of people for whom this is true, while professing values like those of work or the family, means that one tolerates a not insignificant group which has no stake in the accepted general values. If one tolerates a group which has no stake in the accepted general values, one cannot be surprised if people at the margin, and many others, increasingly cast doubt on these values and the values themselves begin to become much more tenuous and precarious than is sustainable for any length of time.

I never argued that football hooligans are themselves a part of the underclass, but I did argue that football hooliganism and similar phenomena, including many of the breaches of law and order in our cities, express a disdain for prevailing values which is legitimised by a society that tolerates a group which is excluded from many of its areas of participation, and from many of its basic rights of participation. So my argument would not be that the underclass is going to march on Westminster or start a new class war; but that the underclass is the living doubt in the prevailing values which will eat into the texture of the societies in which we are living. In fact, it has already done so, which is why there is a very strong moral case for doing something about it.

Policies to meet this challenge
Finally, there are two ways of dealing with a phenomenon like the category called underclass. One is to try and make them a part of the official society, and here I am sure the key is education rather than church membership. That is to say I would send teachers

rather than missionaries to the inner cities to try and persuade people to accept the usefulness of elementary skills. As we have heard this morning, qualifications are crucial in order to be a part of the labour market and, perhaps more than the labour market, of the social universe in which we are living.

Beyond that, I feel very strongly that the values of citizenship have a lot of power in them, and citizenship means that human beings have certain entitlements as members of the society in which we are living. In this connection, I believe that one of these entitlements should consist in basic income guarantees. I am, of course, aware of the Seattle and Denver studies to which David Willetts referred, and to the fact that they have demonstrated certain adverse effects of guaranteed incomes; but it still seems to me that extending the notion of citizenship to this area of social participation is very much in line with the kind of values which I foresee as being dominant once we have abandoned the emphatic insistence on either work or the traditional family as dominant values of our society. However, I say this with considerable hesitation and with the sure knowledge that even a society which is genuinely based on citizenship values will have its dropouts and in that sense its underclass.

6   Policy Issues and the Underclass Debate

James Cornford

I am sceptical of claims that the identification of an underclass will provide any useful clues about how to deal with poverty, unemployment, underemployment, poor health, poor education, homelessness, disorder, or any of the other problems with which it has been associated. *Institutional* definitions of the underclass such as that proposed by W G Runciman,[1] include many such as the elderly, the sick or the disabled, who are not critical to the *political* notion of an underclass: that there are significant numbers of people whose own attitudes and behaviour exclude them from the labour market; whose attitudes and behaviour may be reinforced by the receipt of social security benefits; whose example may influence others, particularly their own children; and whose existence alienates respectable taxpayers and therefore jeopardises support for those who genuinely need and deserve it. Two things are striking about the debate on this political underclass: the extent to which definitions have to be narrowed in order to isolate those whose behaviour is seen to be threatening; and secondly the elusiveness of the group even when the definitions are narrowed, as previous papers in this symposium have suggested.[2] The spectre of the undeserving poor returns to haunt us in different forms; the residuum in the 1890s, social defectives in the 1920s, the problem family in the 1950s, the cycle of deprivation in the 1970s, – whose common theme is the attempt to find an endogenous cause for poverty, whether moral, genetic or social or some combination of the three.[3] The recurrence of the theme suggests both its plausibility and its political importance. The evidence however suggests that while there are people who fit the underclass stereotype (or political definition), they do not constitute a large proportion of the underclass institutionally defined.[4] In the debate on the underclass much attention and anxiety is focused on single parent families, and it is true that such families have a high probability of living in poverty. It is *also* true that four times as many married couples with children live in poverty. The idea of an underclass has a strong political resonance, which partly reflects the familiar and reassuring tactic of blaming the victim.[5] It also provides a means of expressing in terms of poverty and demands on social security concern about ethnic, religious and cultural differences which are disturbing to the majority for other reasons. While in the 1970s and 1980s Western European countries shared similar experiences in the impact of increased unemployment and increased poverty on their programmes of social security, their responses differed markedly with the visibility of the groups affected.[6]

There are anxieties, fears, resentments and prejudices which can be mobilized behind policies directed at the underclass. It is unlikely however that the effects of these policies will be confined to those who ought in theory to be affected, whatever care the proponents may take in their design. It is much more likely that such policies, which are intended to discourage bad behaviour, will make worse the problem they are supposed to overcome, namely the exclusion of those who experience poverty from the wider moral community. Critics of such policies in the United States point to an increasing divide between the majority, who are the recipients of social insurance, and the poor minority who are recipients of residual social assistance: a division

> into *popular* white middle class programs and *unpopular* poor black and hispanic programs; into education for the mainstream and inferior education for ghetto residents; into adequate housing for most of us and squalid unsafe residences or now no residences at all for the rest. And we increasingly use the residual social assistance programs of AFDC, Medicaid and food stamps to mark those who are different, to signal who are unintegrated. The underclass is only part of this problem and, were it not for the fear engendered by the behavioral characteristics that are, after all, only a self-fulfilling affirmation of our beliefs, most Americans would probably not care very much.[7]

The debate on welfare policies in this country reflects the same themes and the same values as that in the United States, in which the Protestant ethic and the Victorian poor law have combined to make welfare a force for division rather than integration. The underlying emphasis has been that deserving claimants get benefits because they have paid for them, and the rest are deterred from claiming unless they are desperate. Hence that other demon of welfare 'the scrounger', the individual version of the underclass. The explicit aim of policy in the 1980s has been to target social security on those most in need. The case is usually made in terms of the best use of resources, but in practice it becomes *morally* discriminatory because it involves differentiating between those who *really* need help from those whose poverty is their own fault. The realities of targeting raise the question of whether enforceable rights can ever be incorporated into a system based on means-testing. It is not clear for instance that benefits depending on statutory entitlement rather than discretion have actually provided claimants with a greater sense of their rights to claim benefits, though the growth of the welfare rights movement suggests that it may be easier for others to claim on their behalf. Many still believe that decisions are at the discretion of DSS officers, and the take-up rates for those benefits, particularly for family credit, suggest that ignorance of entitlement and the stigma attached to claiming remain barriers, despite extensive advertising.

It is more important however to recognise that targeted benefits cannot tackle poverty and disadvantage because they come into play too late in the cycle. There is no preventive component to means-testing because claimants have to be 'poor' in order to qualify. It could indeed be argued that means-testing in itself consolidates dependency and discourages thrift.

It is also within the mean-tested income scheme (supplementary benefit until 1988, now income support) that there are clear examples of groups of claimants who have been actively discriminated against in the application and administration of existing legislation:

> Operation Major in Oxford involved a highly publicised swoop by the police on single homeless claimants allegedly involved in fraudulent bed and breakfast claims. While the claimants were subjected to humiliating procedures and subsequent prosecution, the bogus landlords who had been making the real money were not punished.

- Lone parents are subject to surveillance and interrogation to prove that they are not cohabiting. In the mid 1980s, special fraud teams were drafted into local DSS offices to target single parents.
- There is considerable evidence of discrimination against black claimants. The latest report from NACAB cites examples of such things as requiring these claimants to produce unnecessary written evidence and information to support their claims.[8]

Recent legislative changes to means-tested benefits have also provided the occasion both for the withdrawal of benefits and for justificatory attacks on the moral entitlement of certain groups to benefit. One example was the decision in 1988 to end entitlement to income support for 16 and 17 year olds and to pay reduced rates of benefit to 18 to 25 year olds; another has been the debate in 1990 around the single parent's right to claim benefit, related to the question of how to ensure that fathers pay towards the upkeep of their children. The safety net of means-tested benefits is one in which people get enmeshed: it is not a trampoline from which they can readily and confidently expect to spring back to independence.

The role of social security
The question then is whether the social security system can be itself be an effective instrument for reducing poverty and disadvantage. Much depends here on how we view the future of work or whether we believe that in our society non-employed claimants of working age can ever achieve an adequate income, self-esteem or a sense of being part of mainstream society. Early retirement is a good test of the problem. It would clearly be attractive to many people to retire early if they could count on sufficient income. It is an altogether less attractive prospect if income from benefits will always be lower than income from earnings and if early retirement in reality means early entry into low income, low status and social isolation.

A more difficult question in the 1990s is what benefits should be available to people in paid work. The idea that social security should be a replacement income for earnings and that earnings would provide an adequate income for workers has been seriously undermined in the 1980s. The experience of the last ten years has left us with almost as many poor people trapped in low paid work as on benefits. What the low income figures do not reveal are the movements between these groups. There is evidence that some people move between non-employment and precarious jobs, casual or part time and become trapped in a low income cycle from which it is increasingly difficult to break out.[9] If nothing is done through training and labour market strategies to improve the opportunities of these people and their children, to improve their skills and job prospects, then social security policy may consolidate the position of the working poor. There remains the question of whether wage supplementation through the social security system is either desirable or effective.

But there are changes that could be made to the social security system to reduce discrimination against some non-employed claimants. Different groups of claimants are subject to different conditions of entitlement and forms of administration and qualify for different levels of benefit:

Levels of benefit
Why should an unemployed person receive less national insurance benefit (and for a shorter period) than someone who is sick? The system could be made simpler and more inclusive

if all claimants regardless of status received the same weekly rate of non-means-tested benefit.

Conditions of entitlement

There is evidence that the ways in which conditions are imposed on claimants, proof of unemployment for instance, are often discriminatory. There is a growing view that entitlement should not depend on a national insurance record. But whether claimants should be able to get benefits without any conditions is much more contentious. There is a real tension between the desire to have a benefit system based on universalism and values of social integration and the doubt that people 'getting something for nothing' could be politically acceptable.

Means-testing

Despite repeated attempts, it has not proved possible to devise a system for means-testing that is not exceedingly complex. Nor has it proved possible to have one standard means test for different benefits and services.

There may be ways to reduce the isolation and discrimination faced by claimants, in part on the lines promised in the Government's Citizens Charter. But any welfare strategy which increases the role of means-testing is going to put more people into the poverty trap, increase welfare dependency and thus also increase the political visibility and vulnerability of the poor. We need to find ways to reduce dependence on means-testing.[10]

All this becomes more important in the light of current economic trends. The triumph of capitalism, or the market economy, has not included the elimination of the trade cycle. Conventional wisdom suggests that the integration of the world economy and rapid technological change involve running our economy with a much higher level of unemployment than we imagined tolerable twenty years ago, and a growth of precarious, casual and unskilled work in the service sector. With the aim of overcoming labour market rigidities, Government policies have reinforced these trends. Employment rights such as protection against unfair dismissal and maternity provisions have been watered down and their coverage reduced: public services have been contracted out to private firms whose conditions of employment are much worse than those in the public sector; other government services have been privatised which has removed the low paid from the coverage of collectively negotiated agreements; wage protecting conventions such as the fair wage resolution and Schedule 11 have been abolished; and the wages councils, introduced to set legally binding minimum wages in low wage sectors, have had their powers reduced and are threatened with abolition.[11] Social security policy cannot deal with these problems, but they underline the importance of a system that is designed to sustain the precariously employed, rather than subject them to increasingly harsh tests of availability for work or reduce eligibility for out of work benefits.

Education and training

I do not mean to suggest that we must take the current level of unemployment as given. But the room for manoeuvre in economic policy has certainly been reduced, particularly by membership of the EC and the Exchange Rate Mechanism, so that 'Keynesianism in one country' is no longer an option. We have to look to investment, innovation and training both to create more jobs and to equip people better to do them. Nobody now needs to be told that education and training must be a national priority; the question is what are the right prescriptions. After a brief look at that, I shall return more directly to the position of children, whose experience and development are at the core of anxieties about the underclass.

The education system fails the lower half of the ability range and was designed to do so. Public examinations have been a device for rationing opportunity and reflect the needs of the academic minority. These things are changing, with much hand-wringing about standards and excellence and much abuse of the teaching profession, the essential agent for any improvement. But careful comparisons of levels of achievement with other countries make it plain beyond doubt that, for the non-academic, standards of education and training are lower than for their counterparts in Germany or Japan.[12] This is not because standards have been falling but because they have not been rising fast enough to match changes in the labour market and were in any case conceived on the wrong model: academic excellence for the few, a watered down version for the rest. Reforming the education system is not just about raising standards but about rethinking the standards we are trying to achieve.[13] It is doubtful that the changes introduced by the Education Reform Act of 1988 will do either: the National Curriculum is too ambitious, too prescriptive, and too conventional in its conception. It was also overloaded and is having to be revised. It has not addressed the problem of the persistent neglect of practical and vocational training as an element in the education of all children. It has at least the dignity of a forlorn hope, launched with good intentions but incapable of implementation in its original form. The second major innovation of the Act was the introduction of a quasi market among schools, with the intention that competition for pupils should drive up standards. This may well have the effect of raising morale and achievement in particular schools: that it will have the same effect across the school system is difficult to believe. Indeed it is hard to credit that as the real motive behind the policy.[14] What we need now is an unequivocal commitment to guarantee a place in education and/or training to every pupil up to the age of 18; and a thorough reappraisal of the relation between education and training at all stages and levels of the system. Finally we need to encourage experiment and diversity, which can only happen in a system which is locally led and managed, which is responsive to local conditions and capable of effecting collaboration in practice between the relevant institutions. This implies a restoration of the role of local education authorities and clearer relationships between them and the bodies charged with responsibilities for training.

Children and family

The debate on the underclass has been greatly concerned with the single parent, bringing up children on her own, frequently on benefit, unemployed and poor. The lone parent has become the focus, almost the scapegoat, for trends in domestic life about which there is understandably great concern. These trends suggest that in the future fewer people will marry; more couples will choose to live together without marrying; more children will be born to such couples; that between a third and two fifths of new marriages will end in divorce; and hence that more children will grow up in lone-parent families. For the most part this will not happen because of a deliberate choice by women to bring up children on their own, but because of separation and divorce. Since the breakdown of the traditional family is blamed for many of the social problems associated with the underclass – poor performance of children at school or work, delinquency, violence, crime and sexual abuse, it is worth observing that these problems are not confined to single-parent families:

> Most domestic violence and child sexual abuse is perpetrated by married men against their own wives and children... The great majority (84%) of adults convicted of

criminal offenses are male; and men account for an even higher proportion (91%) of those convicted of violent crimes. Many of these male convicted criminals are married men and it is undoubtedly the case that many boys learn to be violent and/or criminal by following the example of their own fathers.[15]

While recent studies confirm the commonsense observation that many problems in youth have their origins in poor upbringing, it is less clear that this reflects the structure of families rather than the fact that many parents in all kinds of families are ill equipped to provide the security, affection and discipline which enable children to flourish. What we can say with more confidence is that poverty makes the job of parents infinitely harder. However much we may deplore current trends it seems to me unlikely that public policy will do much to reverse them: and if that is attempted by deterrence or punishment, it will succeed only in visiting the sins of the parents upon their children (unto what generation?). The aim of policy should be to mitigate the failures of the family, however they occur, and in particular to enable women to escape from the dependency and isolation to which the sole care of young children often reduces them.

Childcare

One essential element in any strategy to increase the independence of women must be an improvement in the provision of childcare. Present provision is inadequate and haphazard, and more readily available to the better off than to those who need it most. A recent cost benefit analysis of three national schemes of varying scale suggests that any of them would enable many of the immediate users to improve their incomes, but that the Treasury would also see a net benefit from increased taxation and a reduction in social security payments.[16]

Employment

For those in work there are also changes which would make it easier to combine jobs and child rearing: more generous maternity leave, paternity leave and parental leave to cope with family crises would all help to enable working women and their spouses to cope more effectively with family responsibilities. Since in more and more families both parents work, it is important not only to stress the joint responsibility for child rearing, but to provide male workers with similar rights to leave, so that they *can* take their share of responsibility and the burden is not placed entirely upon the woman to adjust her working life to domestic responsibilities.[17]

There is however a strong argument for adjusting the organization of working time to suit the needs of the family. Women need not be faced with a choice between full time motherhood or full time work with childcare. Flexible working arrangements should be available without the sacrifice of career prospects, benefits, or employment protection which part-time work usually now entails. The European Commission's draft directives of June 1990 would require that part-time workers be given the same access to vocational training, occupational social services and benefits in cash and kind as full time workers. These proposals are on the right lines: every employee, including those only working a few hours a week, should be protected by social security contributions earning a proportional entitlement to sickness, unemployment and maternity benefits, and a retirement pension. A system of proportional rights and payment of social security would be much more conducive to finding a pattern of work which suits both employers and many female employees.[18]

Income

To those who are concerned about the impact of poverty on children, the defence and improvement of *child benefit* is the single most important policy. It has been variously suggested that child benefit should be taxed, means-tested, abolished and replaced by tax allowances or doubled for children under five but abolished for the rest. All these proposals miss the point: the great strength of child benefit is precisely that it is universal, that it is universally claimed, that it goes directly to the mother and is spent by mothers on their children. It is especially valuable to single parents, since it continues to be paid when the parent takes a job. It is therefore an incentive to be self-supporting, unlike a tax allowance which would be of no help to single parents on benefit and only useful when employed if their earning were high enough to use the full allowance. The aim must be to increase child benefit, but not by cutting it for over fives: many mothers are still at home with children over five and children grow more expensive as they get older. Nor does the proposal to tax child benefit make sense: at lower income levels there would be greatly increased administrative costs for the Inland Revenue in collecting tax and at the higher levels it would be simpler to raise tax rates to compensate.

Most single-parent families live in poverty and this is the most important cause of the low educational achievement and job prospects of their children. For those families income support is too low, but it is also the case that current social security arrangements, and labour market conditions, make it difficult for most single parents to support themselves and their children. The position has recently been made worse. A single parent's child care costs used to be deducted from her part time earnings before benefit was reduced. Since April 1988 benefit has been reduced pound for pound once the mother starts earning and there is no allowance for childcare expenses. This traps most single mothers into dependence on welfare. The aim must be to encourage single parents, especially as their children get older, to escape dependency by allowing deduction of childcare costs, travel and other work expenses, before benefit is reduced, by increasing child benefit, and by offering training.

Child benefit is attractive because it is universal, non contributory, not means tested or taxed, and because it benefits directly those for whose benefit it is intended. It was right to start with children, but if we are to overcome the problem of persistent poverty, which is not a matter of absolute deprivation but of the distribution of wealth at any given time, we have to address ourselves to the question of what is an acceptable minimum for everyone. As Ralf Dahrendorf has put it:

> the principle remains valid that every citizen is entitled to the security of a basic status which is independent of his or her market value. This requires money.

> The questions are: how much? how should it be raised? and how should it be made available. Citizenship demands a system which is universal, non-discriminatory, and simple. In other words neither elaborate methods of targeting, nor the creation of numerous pots for different needs, nor the setting up of a huge bureaucracy are compatible with the intended effect. That is why basic income guarantees and negative income tax mechanisms are so attractive.[19]

Attractive but utopian, since so many schemes appear to founder on the dilemma of too low a guaranteed income against too high a tax rate. The recent publication of James Meade's *Agathopia*[20] is thus particularly welcome because he addresses the distribution of wealth in a fundamental way and works through in detail the means of transition to the better world to which he aspires. He starts from a concern with Labour-Capital partnerships, which allow for the participation in *Capital* by employees in the private sector. To this is added a fiscal regime which encourages saving but taxes inheritance severely, in order to encourage the diffusion of wealth but not its accumulation. He proposes the gradual elimination of all transfer payments and their replacement by a tax free social dividend, closing the gap between child benefit and the pension. This is to be funded in the long term by the social ownership of half the nation's capital by an investment fund: this fund is to act like any other institutional investor and to manage its investments to maximise the social dividend. Not everyone will agree with Meade's prescriptions, but they do have the outstanding merit that he has thought in detail about how to get there.

Imagining the future is important, but does not offer immediate relief: we could greatly alleviate poverty, and reduce the nightmare of an underclass, directly and immediately by reversing many of the policies adopted over the last decade, especially with regard to housing, social security and taxation. We have witnessed an onslaught on the poor and ought to make amends. Where damage has been done and people, especially young people, need personal help, beyond training, work and hope for the future, we should do our best to give it. We have some of the necessary knowledge and skills.[21] What we lack is the political will. We shall not generate that by punishing the shortcomings of the poor.

Notes

1. W.G. Runciman, 'How Many Classes are there in Contemporary British Society?' *Sociology*, Vol.24 No.3, August 1990, p.388 (those members of British society whose roles place them more or less permanently at the economic level where benefits are paid by the state to those unable to participate in the labour market at all).

2. See for instance the discussions by a cautious proponent of the notion in Isabel V. Sawhill 'Poverty and the Underclass' in Isabel V. Sawhill (ed.), *Challenge to Leadership* (Urban Institute, Washington DC, 1990), pp.215-246; and Theodor R. Marmor, Deborah A. Chassman, Elizabeth S. Auld, *A Comparative Perspective on New Poverty and the Underclass* (Institute for Social and Policy Studies, New Haven, 1988).

3. For a review of this theme over the last hundred years see John Macnicol, 'In Pursuit of the Underclass', *Journal of Social Policy* 16, 3, pp.293-318; and for a telling analysis of the Edwardian debate: 'Class and Poverty in Edwardian England' Chapter 6 in Ross McKibbin, *The Ideologies of Class* (Oxford, 1991).

4. E.g. the Urban Institute's definition of the underclass in the US as 'people who live in neighbourhoods where welfare dependency, female headed families, male joblessness and dropping out of high school are all common occurrences', Sawhill op.cit. p.229. In these neighbourhoods by no means all the people are poor; the majority are black or hispanic; three-fifths have less than a high school education; the majority of men are irregularly employed; three-fifths of the households are headed by women; one-third of households are on public assistance. But in 1980 the people in these neighbourhoods constituted only 4 per cent of the poor in US, and while 59 per cent of them were black, these constituted fewer than 6 per cent of the black population and fewer than 20 per cent of the black poor. The ecological component of the political definition, which emphasises concentration, visibility and loss of social control, thus needs to be kept in perspective.

5. See Alan Walker's vigorous attack in Charles Murray, *The Emerging British Underclass* (IEA Health and Welfare Unit, 1990) pp.49-58.

6. Marmor et al., op.cit. passim.

7. Marmor et al., op.cit p.113.
8. National Association of Citizens' Advice Bureaux, *Barriers to Benefits* (January 1991).
9. W.W. Daniel, *The Unemployed Flow* (Policy Studies Institute, London, 1990).
10. David Piachaud, 'Revitalising Social Policy', *The Political Quarterly*, Vol.62 No.2, April-June 1992, pp.210-11; and Lynda Bransbury, *Escaping from Dependency: Welfare Strategies for Working Parents* (Institute for Public Policy Research, forthcoming).
11. S. Deakin and F. Wilkinson, *The Economics of Employment Rights* (Institute of Employment Rights, London, 1990); F. Wilkinson, *Low Pay and the Statutory Minimum Wage* (Institute for Public Policy Research, forthcoming).
12. S. Prais and K. Wagner, 'Schooling Standards in England and Germany', *National Institute Economic Review*, May 1988 and *Productivity, Education and Training: Britain and Other Countries Compared* (National Institute for Economic and Social Research, London, 1989).
13. For an attempt to do this in regard to education from 16 to 19 see David Finegold et al, *A British Baccalauréat: Ending the Division between Education and Training* (Institute for Public Policy Research, 1990).
14. Cf. David Miliband, *Markets, Politics and Education* (Institute for Public Policy Research, 1990).
15. Anna Coote, Harriet Harman and Patricia Hewitt, *The Family Way* (Institute for Public Policy Research, 1990), p.25 and passim, on which the following observations are based.
16. Bronwen Cohen and Neil Fraser, *Childcare in a Modern Welfare System* (Institute for Public Policy Research, 1991).
17. Coote et al, *The Family Way*, pp.48-49.
18. See Susan McRae, *Flexible Working Time and Family Life* (Policy Studies Institute, London, 1989); and Patricia Hewitt, *Working Time* (Institute for Public Policy Research, forthcoming).
19. Ralf Dahrendorf, 'Citizenship and the Modern Social Conflict', in Richard Holme and Michael Elliott (eds), *1688/1988: Time for a New Constitution* (London, 1988) p.121.
20. J.E. Meade, *Agathopia: The Economics of Partnership* (The David Hume Institute, Aberdeen, 1989).
21. See Lisbeth B. Schorr, *Within Our Reach: Breaking the Cycle of Disadvantage* (New York, 1988).

7 Liberty, Poverty and the Underclass
A classical-liberal approach to public policy

David G. Green

Introduction

In this chapter, the term 'underclass' refers to identifiable forms of behavioural change, including the decline of the work ethic, measured in part by entrenched long-term unemployment; the rise in the casual creation of human life, measured in part by illegitimacy statistics; the abandonment of children before they have been fully raised, measured in part by rising divorce and separation involving children; and the rise in anti-social conduct, measured by crime statistics. That is, in this chapter the term underclass refers to particular types of behaviour which are either self-injuring or anti-social, or both. It does not imply a rigid class structure similar to a caste system in which behavioural norms are transmitted infallibly from generation to generation, although the extent of inter-generational transmission of behavioural traits is among the reasons for concern.

Concern about the underclass cannot be separated from the continuing questions which confront free societies, and in particular, how best to maintain a sphere of individual initiative, as well as a moral community and a political community. The state, especially in its capacity as a guardian of justice before the law, is vital, but its powers can be abused. No less important, life in a moral vacuum would be intolerable. But at the same time, moral pressures can also become too invasive and stifle personal liberty. These dilemmas are the perennial problems of any free society. How can the powers of the state and civil society be balanced so that individuals are most free to develop their potential to contribute to the good of all, including themselves? And, how can a moral order be maintained, guarding on the one hand against nihilism, and on the other against deterioration into sheer intolerance?

Maintaining a moral community

A significant impediment to reasoned debate about the underclass is the tendency to conceive the issue in class-war terms, with an accompanying hint of a struggle between good and evil, or in the view of one recent writer, between humanity and efficiency:

> Setting the requirements of humanity in social welfare policies against those of efficiency in the market involves striking a balance between social and economic markets in our mixed economy. That the scales are tipping decisively against humanity

is indicated by recent discussion of the desirability of workfare policies by politicians on the political right.[1]

In the view of some commentators in this tradition, the Thatcher government set out deliberately to widen the gap between rich and poor. Professor Alan Walker, for instance, claims that the creation of a 'rapid and massive polarisation of living standards' has been a 'conscious act of Government policy'.[2] The extremes of severe deprivation and great wealth have, he says, been 'openly engineered' by government.[3] It follows that, if the poor are victims of government policy then to focus on their behaviour is to 'blame the victim'.

The poor, in this view, should not be judged. The counter view is that it is highly problematic for a free society to put some of its citizens outside the judgement of their fellows. Indeed, one of the central claims of the main champions of liberty over the last 200 or more years has been that a free society can only work if we expect a great deal of one another. In this view, there is always a possibility that a free society might disintegrate amidst the selfishness of its members and the ultimate safeguard against such decay is the vigilance of all citizens. The law plays a vital part in preventing disorder, as do the checks and balances and mutual adjustments of both competitive markets and political conflict, but individual conscience is an equally indispensable bulwark of freedom. Indeed, for thinkers like Acton, liberty is to be understood as precisely, 'the reign of conscience' as contrasted with the reign of authority.

The old medieval order was based on authority in all spheres: in religion, the bishops were in charge; in politics, the king dominated; in village life, the lord of the manor or the village meeting narrowed the scope for personal initiative; and in the towns, the guilds dictated all aspects of manufacturing and trade. The seventeenth century saw the beginning of the end of the old order, but it did not put in its place the mere will of individuals. Rather, it replaced the fetters of authority with the conscience of each person, nurtured at first in the family, and then moulded by the criticism or praise of friends, neighbours and associates in all the communal endeavours which make up human life. In this tradition, each owed it to all the others to live their life as an effort to be a better person, that is, as a self-reliant contributor to the common good. As Michael Novak and his co-authors have remarked, free persons demand much of one another: 'The source of the nation's beauty, and of the love its citizens bear it, is that it asks so much of them'.[4]

Consider now some remarks of a few long-term unemployed people, made during interviews conducted for Full Employment UK in November 1989. One man, described as 25-year old Paul from Sydenham, commented:

> The social security haven't got a clue. You can have them over left, right and centre. Now and then I get my giro, go out, spend it, and next day go down and say the giro hasn't come. They say fill a form in, come back at 2.00 and you'll get another one. That's the only way to survive in this world. I do it about once every two months. It's an extra few pence.[5]

He explained how he earned about £250 a week 'on the side' for at least eight months of the year. Others showed similar attitudes when asked about the 'actively seeking work' regulations. Adam, a 21-year old from Rochdale, who had been unemployed for two years said: 'Whatever they do to us, we can find a way round it, and we do'. Twenty-year old Claire, who had been unemployed since leaving school four years earlier said: 'If they blag us, we can blag them'. And 49-year old Douglas from Cheltenham, who had been unemployed for seven years, said: 'They set up the system, we've learnt how to use it. That's what it's all about'.[6]

The advocate of non-judgementalism would be reluctant to find fault with the views of these unemployed people. But are we truly powerless to criticise such attitudes? How long, for instance, would freedom survive if such opinions were the norm? Human dignity demands that we expect much of ourselves and of others. Membership of a free community is precisely to be part of a circle concerned to improve the quality of life for all by common endeavour and by mutual praise and criticism. To put some people beyond criticism or praise is to put them outside the community. It is almost to write them off as not worth bothering with.

The proper province of the state

The underclass question cannot be divorced from the debate about the proper role of the state. Allow me first to quote at length from J.S. Mill's *Principles of Political Economy* and to ask whether Mill's views are still relevant. In the passages about to be quoted he is attempting to elucidate the principles which should determine the proper scope of government. For him, the purpose of the state should be to make possible the liberty of its people, and government action should, therefore, be the exception and private initiative the rule. And he was clear that, even when certain functions must be undertaken by government because people are incapable of performing them, the state must nevertheless seek to liberate its citizens:

> the mode in which the government can most surely demonstrate the sincerity with which it intends the greatest good of its subjects, is by doing the things which are made incumbent on it by the helplessness of the public in such a manner as shall tend not to increase and perpetuate, but to correct the helplessness. A good government will give all its aid in such a shape as to encourage and nurture any rudiments it may find of a spirit of individual exertion... Government aid, when given merely in default of private enterprise, should be so given as to be as far as possible a course of education for the people in the art of accomplishing great objects by individual energy and voluntary co-operation.[7]

To understand the relevance of Mill's approach to today's debate it may be helpful to distinguish between three theories of the state: *protector*, *liberator*, and *provider*. Mill was opposed to the narrowly limited view of the state as *protector* urged, for instance, by the Manchester school, whose members were content that the state should confine itself largely to defence against foreign enemies and to the prevention of crime. On other issues, they urged non-interference. For many in the classical-liberal tradition this was not enough. Acton, for example, recoiled strongly from strict non-interference when applied to factory legislation. The Ten Hours Bill was opposed by the Manchester school in the 1840s partly because it was asserted that there should be no interference in the contract between worker and employer, and partly because they believed the cost of compliance would enable foreign competitors to undercut home manufacturers. Passed in 1847, the Act limited the hours of work of all between the ages of 9 and 18 to ten hours a day, excluding meals.[8] Acton criticised the opponents of the Bill for putting the interests of manufacturers before liberty. For him, to see liberty as merely about non-interference was inadequate.[9] T.H. Green, who is often claimed by collectivists as a source of inspiration, took a similar view. Writing in 1881, he questioned the extent to which freedom of contract should be tolerated: 'freedom of contract, freedom in all the forms of doing what one will with one's own, is valuable only as a means to an end. That end is... freedom in the positive sense: in other words, the liberation of the powers of all men equally for contributions to a common good.' For this reason he thought that restrictions might have to be placed on labour contracts 'to prevent labour from being sold under conditions which make it impossible for the person selling it ever to become a free contributor to social good in any form'. This, he said, 'is most plainly the case when a man bargains to work under conditions fatal to health'.

For J.S. Mill, too, the state should be a *liberator*, seeking to set loose the energies and initiative of its people. But he was opposed to the state taking on the role of *provider*, making provision for all our principal material requirements. Such a state could only deny human potential. Early this century L.T. Hobhouse distinguished as clearly as any thinker between the liberator and provider states. According to Hobhouse, who shares with T.H. Green the distinction of being well regarded by collectivists, the provider state drew on two socialist traditions which he called 'mechanical socialism' and 'official socialism'. Mechanical socialism had three attributes. First, according to Hobhouse, it was based on a false interpretation of history: it attributed the phenomena of social life and development solely to the 'economic factor'. Second, it supposed a class war, resting on an exaggeration of the distinction between classes. Third, it proceeded by the construction of a utopia which made insufficient provision for 'liberty, movement and growth'.[10] Official socialism began with what he called a contempt for 'ideals of liberty based on a confusion between liberty and competition'; and proceeded from there 'to a measure of contempt for average humanity in general'. It saw humankind as 'a helpless and feeble race' which should be treated in a kindly manner. Of course, true kindness, continued Hobhouse, 'must be combined with firmness, and the life of the average man must be organised for his own good'.[11] Socialism so conceived, believed Hobhouse, has 'nothing to do with democracy or with liberty'.[12]

Hobhouse preferred his own brand of liberalism, which had two properties. First, it must be democratic, that is it must grow from below, not from above. Second, 'It must give the average man free play in the personal life for which he really cares.'[13] It must make for the development and not the suppression of personality, that is, its aim should be to secure 'the conditions of self-maintenance for the normal healthy citizen.'[14] His concern was not to bring about minimal government, nor did he regard all state activity as automatically distasteful. His focus was on the liberty of the individual – not the individual in isolation, but the communal person in mutual concert with friends, neighbours and colleagues. The task of the state was, not to provide for every desire of the people by means of public sector monopolies; it was to liberate them, thereby improving through mutual co-operation what Mill had earlier called their 'moral, intellectual and active worth'.

Summary

I have laboured these distinctions because it is important to recognise that the case for liberty is wider than the case for competition. Competition is concerned with the production of goods and services. Liberty, in the tradition of Acton, is concerned, not only with the balance between the powers of the state and the powers of the individuals, but also with the creation and preservation of a moral community. The economic, political and moral spheres are, in this tradition, distinct from one another but not separate. Each interacts with the other.

The difficulty with much contemporary debate about social welfare is that, of the two main schools of thought, one believes that a remedy can be discovered primarily within the political sphere and that moral considerations are inappropriate; whilst the other urges a remedy based on the application of economic principles to welfare policy – in practice adjusting benefit recipients' incentives at the margin. One of the claims of this paper is that neither approach will succeed without a concern to improve our understanding of the varied ways in which a moral community of free persons can be founded and maintained.

Liberty and poverty

Having outlined the wider philosophy behind this analysis, let me now return in a little more detail to the views of J.S. Mill and then to the arguments of the Charity Organisation Society and the 1909 Majority Report of the Royal Commission on the Poor Laws, all of which throw light on today's controversy. Mill first of all dispenses with the view that all help should be left to private charity:

> ...human beings should help one another; and the more so, in proportion to the urgency of the need; and none needs help so urgently as one who is starving. The claim to help, therefore, created by destitution, is one of the strongest which can exist; and there is *prima facie* the amplest reason for making the relief of so extreme an exigency as certain to those who require it as by any arrangements of society it can be made.[15]

This meant that the state should provide relief. But Mill is fully conscious of the dangers of creating undue dependence on others:

> On the other hand, in all cases of helping, there are two sets of consequences to be considered; the **consequences of the assistance itself,** and the **consequences of** *relying* **on the assistance.** The former are generally beneficial, but the latter, for the most part, injurious; so much so, in many cases, as greatly to outweigh the value of the benefit. (Emphasis added.)

This is never more likely to happen, he says, than in:

> the very cases where the need of help is the most intense. There are few things for which it is more mischievous that people should rely on the habitual aid of others, than for the means of subsistence, and unhappily there is no lesson which they more easily learn. The problem to be solved is therefore... how to give the greatest amount of needful help, with the smallest amount of encouragement to undue reliance on it.[16]

But Mill's approach does not belong to the pure "treat 'em mean and keep 'em keen" tradition. He is aware that:

> Energy and self-dependence are... liable to be impaired by the absence of help, as well as by its excess. It is even more fatal to exertion to have no hope of succeeding by it, than to be assured of succeeding without it.

He continues:

> When the condition of any one is so disastrous that his energies are paralysed by discouragement, assistance is a tonic, not a sedative: it braces instead of deadening the active faculties; always provided that the assistance is not such as to dispense with self-help, by substituting itself for the person's own labour, skill and prudence, but is limited to affording him a better hope of attaining success by those legitimate means.

He recognises that:

> In so far as the subject admits of any general doctrine or maxim, it would appear to be this—that if assistance is given in such a manner that the condition of the person helped is as desirable as that of the person who succeeds in doing the same thing without help, the assistance, if capable of being previously calculated on, is

mischievous: but if, while available to everybody, it leaves to every one a strong motive to do without it if he can, it is then for the most part beneficial.[17]

Mill elaborates further:

> Subject to these conditions, I conceive it to be highly desirable that the certainty of subsistence should be held out by law to the destitute able-bodied, rather than that their relief should depend on voluntary charity. In the first place, charity almost always does too much or too little; it lavishes its bounty in one place, and leaves people to starve in another. Secondly, since the state must necessarily provide subsistence for the criminal poor while undergoing punishment, not to do the same for the poor who have not offended is to give a premium on crime. And lastly, if the poor are left to individual charity, a vast amount of mendicity is inevitable.[18]

But, whilst the state should provide a guarantee for all, it was no less important that 'the task of distinguishing between one case of real necessity and another' should be the responsibility of private initiative:

> Private charity can give more to the more deserving. The state must act by general rules. It cannot undertake to discriminate between the deserving and the undeserving indigent... The dispensers of public relief have no business to be inquisitors. Guardians and overseers are not fit to be trusted to give or withhold other people's money according to their verdict on the morality of the person soliciting it; and it would show much ignorance of the ways of mankind to suppose that such persons, even in the almost impossible case of their being qualified, will take the trouble of ascertaining and sifting the past conduct of a person in distress, so as to form a rational judgement on it. Private charity can make these distinctions; and in bestowing its own money, is entitled to do so according to its own judgement... But the administrators of a public fund ought not to be required to do more for anybody, than that minimum which is due even to the worst. If they are, the indulgence very speedily becomes the rule, and refusal the more or less capricious or tyrannical exception.[19]

Two types of kindness

According to C.S. Loch, Mill's sentiments describe the approach of the Charity Organisation Society (COS) and, indeed, helped to inspire its formation in the 1860s.[20] For Loch, Secretary of the COS from 1875 to 1914, the work of charity ought to be more than 'disorganised sentiment'. It should be a counterpart to the state safety net. Mere almsgiving was insufficient, and the charity of the COS required knowledge and the commitment of time to the person being helped. The focus of the COS on the individual has in more recent times been presented as a callous philosophy, but it emphasised the distinction between, on the one hand, the impulsive and undemanding kindness of giving money, and, on the other, the thoughtful and more committed kindness of taking the trouble to discover the full facts and to ensure that the help given was likely to restore independence, wherever possible. Real charity meant time and trouble, not mere almsgiving, hence the focus of the COS on what it called friendly visiting.

The COS was a major force behind the Majority Report of the Royal Commission on the Poor Laws of 1909. The report, according to C.S. Loch who was a prominent member of the Royal Commission, was based on two central principles. The first was that by combining state financial support with practical help and guidance by voluntary organisations, a humane minimum could be maintained without increasing dependency. The second was that there was much room for the introduction of preventive measures, such as unemployment insurance. Here I will focus on the Royal Commission's proposal to divide responsibility between the public and private sectors.

The Majority Report recommended the abolition of the general workhouse and for separate provision of residential relief to be made for different types of need, including children, the aged or infirm, the sick and the able-bodied. It also proposed that the Boards of Guardians be replaced in each county or county borough by a Public Assistance Authority (PAA) which would exercise overall supervision of relief. The actual work of dealing with applications and providing help would be dealt with by Public Assistance Committees (PACs) which initially would coincide with the former poor law unions. The PACs were to administer benefit, but a vital part of their work was to be delegated to Voluntary Aid Committees.

In the area of each Public Assistance Authority a Voluntary Aid Council was to be established, consisting of representatives of charities, the PAA, friendly societies, trade unions, the clergy and others. In turn, it would form Voluntary Aid Committees (VACs), which would aid people in distress referred to them by the PACs. It was intended that the VACs would attempt first to strengthen family ties and local bonds by encouraging family and friends to give support. At the heart of the work of the Voluntary Aid Committees was to be the voluntary worker or friendly visitor, who would visit, assess and offer practical help as well as moral and prudential guidance.

Modern relevance and the american poverty debate

I mention the approach of the Royal Commission on the Poor Laws because it is necessary to go back some decades to find an official discussion of behavioural poverty which does not surrender to the temptation to duck the hard issues. Since World War Two discussions have been characterised by a growing tendency to explain human conduct as a reaction to environmental influences, and from the 1960s by sociological nihilism which debunked traditional values. The outcome was non-judgementalism. However, in the late 1970s and early 1980s the wisdom of 1960s values began to be questioned, at first in America, and later here.

The modern American approach is summed up in *The New Consensus on Family and Welfare*, a report on poverty in America produced by a working group under the chairmanship of Michael Novak which included participants from all points of the political spectrum.[21] Allow me to summarise its approach and to ask whether it is of any relevance to Britain today:

A good society is judged by how well it cares for its most vulnerable members.

No person should be involuntarily poor without others coming to his or her assistance.

No able adult should be allowed voluntarily to take from the common good without also contributing to it.

Low income and behavioural dependency are two quite different problems and require different remedies.

During the 1980s a number of American social policy analysts began to identify what they saw as flaws in welfare programmes. Some poverty, they agreed, could be understood as a lack of income, but they thought that a distinction should be drawn between poverty due to insufficient cash and behavioural poverty. The pursuit of welfare policies based on the image of the beneficiary as a victim was, in the view of critics like Charles Murray, not only failing to remedy poverty, but was causing it to increase.[22] Cash transfers paid without regard to the self-damaging behaviour of some (but not all) welfare recipients fail to solve the problem of the dependent poor. Indeed, such payments reinforce dependency and encourage more people to fall into the same trap.

The new approach can be summarised under five main themes. First, the role of government in creating an economic climate which permits economic growth is considered essential. Policies to assist people to escape from poverty should, therefore, be consistent with economic growth, technical change and progress.

Second, the new consensus asks that the poor should be disaggregated according to the reasons for their poverty: the elderly, able-bodied unemployed, disabled, one-parent. Personal circumstances count and money alone will not cure poverty for all groups. People who are poor due to self-damaging conduct – the underclass – live in a condition worse than one of low income alone. At the same time, it is recognised that there are many people, such as the frail elderly and the mentally disabled, who should continue to receive generous benefits.

Third, the makers of the new consensus focus on understanding the personal life strategies which have proved successful in enabling people to escape from poverty. They are, therefore, especially interested in people who began life in a bad environment, perhaps with a broken family, much neighbourhood crime, surrounded by drugs and alcoholism in abundance, but who nevertheless escaped. What is it, they asked, that enabled some who started with disadvantages to escape and how are they different from those who did not escape? Their conclusion is that the probability of remaining in poverty is low for those who follow three rules: first, complete high school; second, once an adult, get married and stay married (even if not at the first attempt); and third, stay employed, even if at a wage and under conditions below their ultimate aims. For the able-bodied who require welfare, the focus of policy should be on getting people back to work by means of a discharge plan or independence plan which incorporates the lessons learned by those who have successfully risen above their humble origins. Welfare should be temporary.

The fourth distinctive element is a focus on moral/cultural institutions. The new consensus asks why it is that tried-and-tested methods of self-improvement are not being followed by the 'underclass'. This leads to an examination of the institutions which reinforce without compelling patterns of behaviour, such as the church, voluntary institutions and the family. Traditionally, such institutions, and especially the family have taught values like personal responsibility, hard work, duty, and integrity, but in the 1960s and 1970s self control and impulse restraint were debunked. Morality came to be called convention and defiance of convention began to be admired along with self-expression. The cost of debunking ordinary values like hard work, duty, integrity and self-discipline, say the authors of *The New Consensus on Family and Welfare*, has been borne disproportionately by the poor. A central concern of social policy, they claim, should be to maintain the good health of families because the family is central to the moulding of good character.

These ideas should be distinguished from 'culture of poverty' theories, and particularly the 'cycle of deprivation' theory of poverty, which treated people as if they were largely or wholly the creatures of their circumstances and upbringing. For writers like Charles Murray and Michael Novak, people are at once social animals, much affected by upbringing, incentives and cultural mores, and also free moral agents capable of rising above their circumstances. What interests Murray and Novak is how people who started life under huge disadvantages in fact triumphed over them. This pattern of escaping from poverty by hard work and moral probity is a stronger image in American minds than the

British because Americans can readily recall the waves of poor immigrants who arrived in the USA keen to make the most of the opportunities it offered. Indeed, the very symbol of America, the Statue of Liberty, enjoins the world to 'Send me your tired, your poor, your huddled masses'.

Although this tradition has a stronger resonance in America than in Britain, it is nonetheless relevant because the last 30 years have seen the arrival of substantial numbers of immigrants from the West Indies, India and Pakistan. The last two groups have prospered, although the West Indian experience has been more patchy, almost certainly because the mutual aid of the family is less strong in certain sections of that community.

Fifth, the spokesmen for the new consensus are also distinguished by their desire to re-create a two-sided ideal of self-reliance and community. The images they invoke are again drawn from American history. They picture settlers breaking new ground, working for themselves and their families but all turning out to help both family and neighbours to build barns, schools and churches. Each was self-reliant but also a contributor to the common welfare. This ethic of personal responsibility combined with a personal sense of obligation to render service for the good of all is, they believe, essential to a fulfilled life. The relevance of this belief is that our thinking about welfare policy should embrace both self-reliance and community. To give benefits without imposing obligations is one-sided and treats people as less than full citizens.

Thus, they urge a new conception of self-reliance and community in place of the one-sided doctrine of rights. Instead of seeing people as the bearers of rights or claims on the public purse, people are seen as contributors to the common welfare. Someone who fails to support himself also renders himself incapable of giving service to others. They urge that welfare recipients be viewed, not as victims of circumstance, but as potentially free, responsible, choosing, valuing citizens who need temporary help in order to restore them to fully functioning citizenship. To send them cheques through the post, and no more, is to fail to respect them. To direct attention to the flaws in their own conduct, however, is to respect them as capable of more and thus to encourage an increase in self esteem. Government almsgiving keeps people going, but for most breadwinners no amount of insistence that the cheque is sent as a human right will give them the self-esteem that comes from supporting their families by their own efforts or the self-fulfilment that flows from surviving in the face of challenges in the workplace.

Some proposals for public policy
Guiding assumptions
There is an important difference between low income and behavioural poverty, and in recent years there has been an increase in the number of people in Britain dependent on welfare benefits as a result of their own values and behaviour. This development has been reinforced by the materialistic focus of welfare policy on money transfers alone, and will not be overcome unless we develop an alternative welfare strategy. The next few pages tentatively suggest some possible means of developing a new approach aimed at restoring the dependent poor to independent citizenship. It has four main elements: a focus on personal independence planning; a recognition that the family is central to personal independence; policies aimed at economic growth; and the removal of public-policy obstacles to family or personal advancement.

Personal independence planning

The remedy for behavioural poverty is not bigger welfare benefits, but to devise programmes which focus on the special circumstances of the behaviourally poor, including the skills available to them, their personal conduct, values and morale. The purpose of the new programmes would be to help able-bodied recipients of welfare benefits to achieve that independence of mind and spirit necessary to become contributing citizens. It goes without saying that the emphasis on restoring people to the workforce does not apply to the non able-bodied.

Removal of public-policy impediments

Some public policies, directly or indirectly, narrow opportunities to escape from poverty. Particular culprits are high taxes on incomes and savings, and the inadequate integration of taxes and benefits. A comprehensive reform programme is necessary to remove the impediments which make it more difficult for the poor to advance by their own endeavours.

Bolstering the family

The family is the basic building block of a free society and much has happened in recent years to undermine its vital role in raising children. Moreover, a good deal of today's poverty is the result of family breakdown. The new focus on personal independence will only work if there is an adequate emphasis on the role of the family.

Economic growth

The focus on individual conduct and morals is indispensable to success, but on its own will not be sufficient. Economic growth is a necessary, but not a sufficient, pre-condition for the creation of opportunities to escape from poverty.

Personal independence planning

The government's strategy for the long-term unemployed has been to enforce the 'genuinely seeking work rule', and to introduce Jobclubs, Jobstart, Restart and Job Interview Guarantees, all of which are designed to channel the long-term unemployed into work or training. In addition, training, including the one and two-year Youth Training Schemes, has been re-organised under the new Training and Enterprise Councils. In May 1991 these arrangements were supplemented by the experimental Training Voucher Scheme. Government policy is already moving towards an individually-oriented approach to the restoration of independence and the proposals in this paper advocate an extension and intensification of this strategy.

At present someone signing on as unemployed is called in for a 45-minute interview with a New Client Adviser, whose task it is to advise on job-search techniques and to devise a Back to Work plan. Job Clubs are available, providing free telephone and postage and access to typewriters and stationery and the Jobstart scheme can ease the transition between unemployment and work. After six months unemployment a person is called for a Restart interview to discuss their progress. A further Restart interview follows at twelve months. Week-long Restart courses are made available, offering training in work skills and job search activities such as interview technique. Failure to attend such a course can lead to loss of one week's benefit.

These measures have enjoyed some success, particularly Jobclubs. Restart, however, focuses narrowly on jobs and training, rather than on the full circumstances of the individual. Moreover, it is mistrusted by many intended beneficiaries, according to an independent report by Full Employment UK.[23] Nor is it as successful as it might have been. A survey produced by the Department of Employment found that five months after their initial Restart interview, 55 per cent were still unemployed and after ten months, 44 per cent remained out of work. Of the total, 42 per cent had been continuously unemployed.

The focus on individually-tailored help and advice is highly desirable but, as J.S. Mill had recognised, it seems unlikely that government departments can ever be the best instrument for such work. An alternative approach would be to transfer programmes intended to help particular individuals back into the workforce to private agencies, whether charitable organisations or mutual aid associations. A possible arrangement would be for government departments to refer individuals on benefit to private care associations, which would be charged with devising an 'independence plan' for each person. This independence or 'escape' plan would embrace all aspects of the individual's circumstances relevant to rising out of poverty, including proposals for acquiring workplace skills through training, as well as attention to personal morale, self-esteem and family structure.

This 'independence counselling' should take place against a public policy background of encouraging economic growth in order that the opportunities are there for people to seize, and it should be accompanied by systematic efforts to remove obstacles or impediments to self-reliance created by public policies.

Removal of public-policy impediments
Independence impact assessments
Alongside the independence planning programmes, all current taxes, benefits, regulations, laws and relevant public policies, and all proposals to reform them, should be subject to 'independence impact assessments' to gauge their effect on efforts by individuals to escape from poverty by their own endeavours.

These assessments should include examination of impediments to labour mobility, such as restrictive council-house letting rules, the severe decline in the private rental sector due to rent control and other regulations which deter people from letting their property, and mortgage interest relief subsidies which tend to increase house prices, thus putting home ownership beyond the reach of the less-well paid.

Taxation policy should be subject to especially close scrutiny. Tax thresholds should be raised to allow workers to keep more of their earnings and child tax allowances should be restored as part of a general raising of tax thresholds and in order to bolster the traditional two-parent family. The mutual support of the family still remains the best foundation for independence, a matter to which I return below.

All saving is desirable and should not be penalised, but taxation of interest on savings has an especially harmful effect on those who want to improve their conditions by saving from earnings. Not only does the taxation of interest on savings make it more difficult to escape from poverty, it also reduces the general propensity to save, and thus explains in part why Britain's 'savings ratio' is low by international standards. If all taxation of savings can not be abolished in the short run, the immediate introduction of a tax-free allowance of, say, £5,000 a year not dissimilar to the capital gains tax allowance would be feasible. Since the capital gains tax allowance is already in place, but is unused by the great majority of people, it might be appropriate to redesignate it a dual 'capital gains or interest on savings allowance', in order to benefit everyone and not only the minority who make capital gains.

The family

A free, pluralistic and democratic society can only work if its citizens show self-restraint and tolerance, and display that consideration for others which is vital if the poor and unfortunate are not to go in want. The family has always been, and remains, the best environment in which the skills and moral qualities vital to democracy are acquired. It is, therefore, proper for the government to bolster the family. Yet, public policy in recent years has not consciously sought to reinforce the family. On the contrary, much has happened, sometimes inadvertently, to undermine it.

What policies should the government follow? First it should attempt to undo some of the damage caused in recent years by changes in public policy. Second, it should introduce measures to encourage the traditional two-parent family. This would involve changes in divorce law, reform of the benefits and special advantages available to one-parent families, and revision of the tax treatment of traditional two-parent families.

At the same time it must be recognised that government can only achieve so much, and that without an accompanying change in private attitudes, little will be accomplished. But the government can give a lead in the hope that it may stimulate a spontaneous re-awakening of commitment to the family, offering people an ideal of parenthood, both fatherhood and motherhood, against which to measure themselves. Here is a role for voluntary organisations including the church.

Family impact assessments

Taxes, benefits, the laws and public policy should be subject to 'family impact assessments' to gauge their effect on family stability. Without strong families, behavioural poverty will not be overcome. The importance of the family can be seen from the experience of Indian and Pakistani immigrants to Britain. Many arrive with few material resources, but by hard work and making full use of the human capital of all family members in small retail or manufacturing businesses, they invariably achieve prosperity within a few years.

Divorce

An early target should be divorce law. In recent years, divorce has been made much easier and now all that is required is the consent of both partners, even when children are involved. During the last 20-30 years it began to be thought that an unhappy marriage was bad for children and that it was, therefore, much better for the parents to divorce. Mundane experience had long taught the opposite, that insecurity and the absence of a parent were bad for a child's development, but policy makers were influenced by research which seemed not to support common-sense lessons. However, the truth of the traditional view is now being borne out by recent evidence which suggests that children suffer terribly during divorce.[24] It now appears preferable that the law should encourage unhappy couples to make their marriage work for the sake of their offspring.

Current thinking about divorce, especially divorce by simple mutual consent, also sends the wrong moral message to young people. It shouts aloud that selfishness is fine even when the emotional and practical costs to those who are closest to you are very high. If we applied that attitude generally in our political and working lives it is doubtful whether Britain would remain a tolerant and democratic society for long.

The traditional approach to divorce was to require one partner to show that the other was at fault and the most common grounds for divorce were adultery, desertion and cruelty. This was the principle that applied until the 1969 Divorce Reform Act was enacted. After the 1969 Act, a divorce could be obtained without showing fault, by demonstrating that 'an irretrievable breakdown' of the marriage had taken place. This could be shown by proving one of five facts: adultery, unreasonable behaviour, desertion for two years, that the couple had been separated for two years and both consented to divorce, and that they had been separated for five years, regardless of consent. The significance of this Act was that it removed the moral basis of marriage. The law no longer took a moral stand in favour of sound marriage. Subsequent laws have relaxed the position still further, particularly in 1984 when divorce was permitted after only one year of marriage, instead of three.

Table 7.1   Decrees Absolute granted in the UK

Year	Number	Divorces per thousand married people[*]
1971	80,000	6.0
1976	136,000	10.1
1981	157,000	11.9
1986	168,000	12.9
1988	166,000	12.8

Source: *Social Trends*, 1990, Table 2.15.

*   England and Wales.

In 1987 there were 12.6 divorces per 1,000 existing marriages in the UK. This is significantly higher than the European average of about 7.0 per 1,000.

Table 7.2   Divorce in the EC, 1987

	Divorces per 1,000 existing marriages
Belgium	7.8
Denmark	12.7
France	8.5
Germany	8.8
Ireland	nil
Italy	1.8

Source: *Social Trends*, 1990, Table 2.14

The trend towards the removal of all moral content in divorce law continues. Although divorcing couples are under no obligation to show fault in their partner, in practice the most common 'facts' used to prove 'irretrievable breakdown' are unreasonable behaviour and adultery. The Law Commission, in a report published in 1990, proposes to go still further and to remove the opportunity to divorce on such grounds.[25]

According to this report, divorce will continue to be granted when a marriage has irretrievably broken down, but this state of affairs will be demonstrated by one fact alone, namely that a year has elapsed since the couple officially registered that their marriage had deteriorated. Once the breakdown has been officially notified, under the Law Commission's plan, there will be a 'cooling off' period of one year before the divorce can be finalised. During this year it is intended that the couple will contemplate reconciliation and consider the future of their children. The Law Commission report professes concern for the children, but it fails to acknowledge that it might often be to the children's advantage for the parents not to get divorced at all. Instead, the report aspires to bring about a situation in which the parents can 're-negotiate' their relationship calmly and sensibly rather than by fighting in the courts.[26]

A strong case can be made against these plans, especially where children are involved. Not all divorces involve children, and given modern attitudes it would be advisable for the law to draw a distinction between marriages with and without children. But most divorcing couples do have children. Some 56 per cent of divorces in 1987 involved children under 16, accounting for 150,000 youngsters, most of whom were under 10. In nine out of ten divorces the children stay with the mother, and of those instances in which the man adopts a visiting role, contact is broken in half the cases within two years.

Is there a viable alternative to the Law Commission's proposals? Where no children are involved, the law could be left as it is. But where children are concerned, then the law can rightly expect parents to take their responsibility to their own offspring seriously. Children do not ask to be born. It follows that if people have children they should look after them till they are grown up. Human experience is so diverse that exceptions must be allowed, but the exceptions should be rare.

An alternative to the Law Commission's proposals would be to allow divorce involving children under 18 on one ground alone, namely that the children would be better off. The parents' interests would be firmly subordinated to the children's and to ensure that the children's interests overrode the parents' preferences, the burden of proof would be on the parents to show to the satisfaction of a court—possibly a special family court—that the children would benefit. The Law Commission hopes that by making divorce more amicable it can avoid the insecurity and stress which upsets children. It is much more likely that divorce will continue to increase as a result of their proposals causing more, not less, insecurity and suffering. The Law Commission report has a certain appeal, especially in its emphasis on counselling and cooling off, but the counselling should be to help parents come to terms with their responsibilities, not to devise convenient visiting arrangements and divide up the property amicably.

One-parent families

There are now over a million one-parent families. The proportion of all families which are single-parent, has risen from 8 per cent in 1971 to 14 per cent in 1987.[27] The proportion of lone mothers who were divorced is up from 24 per cent in 1971 to 44 per cent in 1987; never-married mothers account for 29 per cent, up from 16 per cent; while the number of separated mothers has fallen from 29 per cent to 19 per cent, and the proportion of widows from 31 per cent to 8 per cent.[28]

Absconding fathers

The first task should be to ensure that men who father children should not be able to escape their responsibility. Ideally, they ought to provide a proper family life for the child, but failing that, they should be required to meet the full cost of the child's upkeep until they leave school or complete full-time education or training, whether or not the mother marries another man. This will ensure that such children have sufficient to live on, and the high level of payments will additionally have a deterrent effect on potential absconding fathers. A strengthened version of the proposed Child Support Agency would be a suitable vehicle for the enforcement of these measures.

Special benefits

One-parent families have developed effective pressure groups which have demanded and won special benefits which add to the relative attraction of becoming a one-parent family, thus encouraging more people to define themselves as single parents. Not every one-parent family is a problem. There are examples of heroic and successful lone parents and there are inadequate two-parent families, but the inescapable fact is that on average the children of single parents do less well in school, are more likely to turn to crime and develop less well physically.[29] In these circumstances public policy should certainly not encourage single parenthood, but at present it does just that by making available additional benefits for lone parents. A preferable approach would be to remove all the special benefits which are payable to single parents, including one-parent benefit. The effect would be that a man or woman living alone with a dependent child would be treated by the benefit system as if they were a single adult and a single child.

In 1991 a lone parent received child benefit of £8.25 plus one parent benefit of £5.60, both tax free. Income Support was paid as follows.

Personal Allowances	per week
single person	
under 18	£23.65
18-24	£31.15
25 and over	£39.65
dependent children	
under 11	£13.35
11-15	£19.75
16-17	£23.65
18	£31.15
lone parent	
under 18	£23.65
18 or over	£39.65
Premiums	
family	£7.95
lone parent	£4.44

The normal earnings disregard is £5.00 per week (of each partner), but for one-parent families the figure is £15.00. Recipients of Income Support also automatically receive Housing Benefit (100 per cent of the rent) and Community Charge Benefit (80 per cent of the charge). If their net income is above the income support level Housing Benefit is reduced by 65p per pound and Community Charge Benefit by 15p per pound. For the purpose of calculating Housing Benefit, the lone parent premium is increased by £6.20 to £9.70. In addition, lone parents can disregard £15.00 of their part-time earnings, instead of £5.00 for a single person or £10.00 for a married couple one of whom is in part-time work. Since October 1990 lone parents not receiving Income Support have been allowed to disregard £25.00 a week in calculating their entitlement to Housing Benefit and Community Charge Benefit.

The present proposals would mean the abolition of one-parent benefit of £5.60, the lone-parent premium of £4.10, and the additional payment of £7.90 paid to 18-24 year olds who are lone parents. To give an example, a lone parent aged 20 with no other income and with two children aged under 11 would receive £60.85 (comprising income support of £46.35 and child benefit of £14.50) instead of £72.85, a reduction of £12.00 per week.

Two-parent families are almost always better than one-parent families for the children and the benefit system should recognise this. The argument against removing one-parent benefit will be that existing one-parent families will experience losses of income and that nothing should be done to harm them. But there is no easy option, and certainly this issue does not present a clear-cut choice between being harsh or being kind. The choice lies between, on the one hand, the impulsive kindness of demanding that cheques be sent through the post without regard to the long run costs, and on the other, the thoughtful kindness of taking into account the long-run and incidental costs of public policies. There is a dilemma, and it is necessary to choose between the *immediately visible* effects on existing one-parent families and the *hidden* costs on future children living with lone parents. Removing the special benefits will mean that there will be fewer children whose lives are blighted by single parenthood and this overrides the minor hardship which will flow from removing the special one parent benefits today. Moreover, to ease the transition for people already receiving one-parent benefit, the payments could be phased out over 2-3 years.

These modifications of financial incentives at the margin will not in themselves be sufficient. The single most important factor is the moral climate in which individuals make the choices that affect their children. Here again, there is an important role for the proposed private care associations to try to help to restore family life and mutual support networks with advice and practical help.

Economic pressure to work

The number of married women going out to work has increased rapidly in recent years. This change has occurred partly because women now have fewer children and partly because the economic pressures on families have changed, largely because of the mounting burden of direct taxation during the 1960s and 1970s. When women choose to work during the hours their children are at school this raises no real public policy questions, but if mothers work instead of spending time with their pre-school children then this may have damaging results, both for the children and the whole community, which call for changes in public policy. Indeed, for most of the post-war period most European governments have taken the view that the family performs a vital role in nurturing and raising the young and have pursued public policies designed to ensure that families have sufficient cash to allow the mother to remain with her children during the pre-school years.

If either a man or a woman chooses to remain childless in order to pursue a career then no public policy issue is raised, but once children have put in an appearance a strong case can be made for putting the children first, even at the expense of the parents' careers.

Traditionally, the man has been the breadwinner and the woman has cared for the children. Men remain overwhelmingly the sole or principal breadwinners, but there is no reason why the government should seek to reinforce any particular division of responsibility between men and women in marriage. Any couple ought to be free to divide the tasks of earning income and caring for their children as they see fit. But, the government ought not to offer special inducements to couples to transfer responsibility for child care to outside child-care agencies.

Moreover, there is no need at all for the Government to encourage anyone back to work through new tax reliefs. If employers want new staff, they can be counted on to provide the incentives. If the Government feels it must take a view about who should be encouraged back to work, it should direct its attention to the re-training of married women whose children have grown up, and to re-training retired people who, with increased longevity, are a huge wasted resource.

One of the most harmful developments since the last war has been the way in which high income taxes and the erosion of tax thresholds have penalised families with young children precisely when financial pressures are at their height. In 1949, the tax threshold for a man, wife and two children under 11 was 98 per cent of the average manual wage. Now such families start paying tax at about 37 per cent of the average manual wage.[30] A more fruitful strategy for the Government would be to raise tax thresholds, thus allowing families to keep more of the fruits of their own endeavours and relieving the pressure on the mother to go out to work. The most efficient solution would be to restore the child tax allowance, at a level equivalent to the full cost of raising a child. From the time income tax was first introduced, Governments always took into account the dependents of the taxpayer, and it was only in the late 1970s that the allowance for dependent children was withdrawn in favour of child benefit. Economic pressure on families could also be relieved by raising child benefit, but the payment of money by requiring mothers to queue up at the Post Office, as if collecting war-time ration coupons, is wasteful and degrading compared with the use of the tax system.

Conclusion

What is the government's responsibility to the poor and how should it be discharged? For most of the post-war years it has been impossible to debate this issue in a dispassionate manner because of the tendency instantly to classify anyone venturing an opinion as either mean or generous. Thus, to favour 'universal' benefits was generous whilst to advocate 'targeted' benefits was mean. There are still too many who see the issue in simple black and white terms and who regard a demand for more 'caring' as an ample intellectual response. But there are now signs of change. Even some collectivists are beginning to express alarm at what they recognise as the dependency-inducing effects of the welfare state.

The tendency to blame personal conduct on the environment or circumstances and to refrain from passing judgement on 'victims' enjoys a measure of support because criticism of the poor can be an excuse for inaction. But the choice is not between action and inaction. It lies between *methods* of action, and specifically between measures that restore the individual's capacity to be a self-reliant contributor, and those that promote quiescent dependence on others.

The challenge today is to discover how we can protect people from extreme hardship without extinguishing their independence. This used to be the accepted aim of public policy until the 1920s and 1930s when poverty began to be re-defined in purely material terms.

If poverty simply meant a lack of money, the obvious solution was to give the poor some cash and the only issue for debate was how much. Before the Second World War this approach did not gain easy acceptance because reformers came up against the spirit of self-reliance which had long been part of the make-up of the British people. No matter how often they were told that benefits were given as of right, welfare beneficiaries continued to feel a sense of lost self-esteem. Reformers called this lower self-esteem 'stigma', and its avoidance came to dominate discussion of poverty policy in the 1960s and 1970s.

The traditional British attitude found expression in those characteristic working class organisations, the friendly societies and trade unions. The trade unions demanded a 'living wage' while the friendly societies provided against hard times by mutual aid. In Britain when the government introduced compulsory social insurance for 12 million persons under the 1911 National Insurance Act, some 9.5 million were already covered by voluntary insurance associations, chiefly the friendly societies. In 1910, the last full year before the 1911 Act, there were 6.6 million members of registered friendly societies, quite apart from those in unregistered societies. The rate of growth of the friendly societies over the preceding thirty years had been rapid and was accelerating. In 1877, registered membership had been 2.8 million. Ten years later it was 3.6 million, increasing at an average of 90,000 a year. In 1897 membership had reached 4.8 million, having increased on average by 120,000 a year. And by 1910 the figure had reached 6.6 million, having increased at an annual average rate since 1897 of 140,000.[31]

These organisations prided themselves on their success in enabling even the lowest paid workers to be independent. Arguing against proposals for a compulsory state pension scheme in 1882, a spokesman for the 600,000-strong Ancient Order of Foresters, pointed out that thrift had succeeded in considerably reducing the number of paupers. The increased facilities for thrift 'afforded to the British Workman by his own peculiar organisations', friendly societies and trade unions, had done much during the previous thirty years to reduce pauperism, he said. They could look forward to the time when pauperism would be reduced to those suffering from 'insanity and contagion' and pointed with pride to the reduction in pauperism since 1849. In that year paupers had comprised 6.2 per cent of the population of England; in 1859, 4.4 per cent; in 1869, 4.7 per cent; and in 1879, only 3.0 per cent. In Scotland the proportion had fallen from 4.0 per cent in 1859 to 2.8 per cent in 1879.[32]

Allow me to close by reproducing a quotation published in my Foreword to Charles Murray's *The Emerging British Underclass*. The issue is not about blame alone, or about making excuses for inaction. It might well be callous to refuse to help someone on the ground that they were the author of their own misfortune. People should be helped whether or not they are to blame, wholly or partly for their own predicament. The important question is *how* they should be helped. In the days when self-help was the norm and the majority joined mutual aid societies to make provision against hard times, callous disregard for the unfortunate was denounced. The Manchester Unity friendly society, a million-strong voluntary association of workers for mutual aid and one of many similar organisations the membership of which far outnumbered that of the trade unions until the Second World War, enjoined its members to combine caring with criticism:

> In extending our charity we must endeavour to distinguish the really deserving, for those who willingly and professionally seek the charity of others forfeit all self-respect, and, in being content so to live, sacrifice personal dignity.

The duty of the Manchester Unity member in such cases was to try to awaken the 'love of independence'. But, this was not a policy of callous disregard:

> those who unworthily seek assistance are not to be neglected if really in distress; the voice of misery, proceed from whence it may, should never be disregarded. However, after relieving the actual wants of these unhappy persons, we should endeavour to raise them from the degradation into which they have fallen, and make them richer in their own esteem. As it is better that ten guilty persons escape than that one innocent should suffer, so it is better that ten undeserving persons be assisted than that one worthy be neglected.

Notes

1. A. Digby, *British Welfare Policy: Workhouse to Workfare* (Faber and Faber, London, 1989) p.131.
2. A. Walker, 'Blaming the victims', p.55, in Charles Murray et al., *The Emerging British Underclass* (IEA Health and Welfare Unit, London, 1990).
3. *Ibid.*, p.56.
4. M. Novak et al., *The New Consensus on Family and Welfare* (American Enterprise Institute, Washington, 1987) p.xvi.
5. Full Employment UK, *Britain's New Underclass: Challenges for the Employment Service* (Report to the Secretary of State for Employment, December 1989), p.6.
6. *Idem.*, p.8.
7. J.S. Mill, *Principles of Political Economy*, Edited by W.J. Ashley (Longmans, Green & Co, London, 1909) p.978.
8. An Act of 1833 already prohibited children under nine from working in the factories.
9. Lord Acton, 'Report on current events, July 1860', in *Essays in the History of Liberty* (Liberty Classics, Indianapolis, 1985) p.490.
10. L.T. Hobhouse, *Liberalism* (Oxford University Press, London, 1964) pp.88-9.
11. *Ibid.*, p.89.
12. *Ibid.*, p.90.
13. *Ibid.*, p.91.
14. *Ibid.*, p.91.
15. J.S. Mill, *Principles of Political Economy*, Edited by W.J. Ashley (Longmans, Green & Co, London, 1909) p.967.
16. Mill, *Principles of Political Economy*, p.967.
17. Mill, *Principles of Political Economy*, pp.967-8.
18. Mill, *Principles of Political Economy*, p.969.
19. Mill, *Principles of Political Economy*, p.969.
20. C.S.Loch, *A Great Ideal and its Champion: Papers and addresses by the late Sir Charles Stewart Loch* (Allen & Unwin, London, 1923) p.192.
21. M. Novak, et al., *The New Consensus on Family and Welfare* (American Enterprise Institute, Washington, 1987).
22. Charles Murray, *Losing Ground: American Social Policy, 1950-1980* (Basic Books, New York, 1984).
23. Full Employment UK, *Britain's New Underclass: Challenges for the Employment Service* (Report to the Secretary of State for Employment, December 1989).
24. E.g. Ann Mitchell, *Children in the Middle: Living Through Divorce* (Tavistock, London, 1985; J.S. Wallerstein and J.B. Kelly, *Surviving the Breakup* (Grant McIntyre, London, 1980).

25. The Law Commission, *Family Law: The Ground for Divorce*, Law Commission No. 192 (HMSO, London, 1990.
26. *Id.*, para.2.21.
27. *Social Trends*, Table 2.7.
28. *Social Trends*, Table 2.8.
29. E.g. I. Kolvin, F.J.W. Miller, D. Scott, S.R.M. Gatzanis, and M Fleeting, *Continuities in Deprivation?: The Newcastle 1000 Family Study* (Avebury, Aldershot, 1990). ESRC/DHSS Studies in Deprivation No.15.
30. *1989 Inland Revenue Statistics* (HMSO, London) Appendix C, p.132.
31. D.G. Green, *Working Class Patients and the Medical Establishment* (Gower/Temple Smith, London, 1985) p.179.
32. *Foresters Miscellany*, January 1882, p.6.

8   The Future of the Underclass

David J. Smith

This conference tried to promote the analytical and empirical approach to thinking about the idea of an underclass in Britain. A number of the contributions have moved the discussion forward by examining evidence on the underclass within the framework of an agreed definition.

The significance of persisting high unemployment
The proposal in Chapter 1 was to define the underclass as those who fall outside the class schema because they belong to family units having no stable relationship with legitimate gainful employment. It was suggested that changes in the life cycle should be taken into account: old age pensioners and students are not part of the underclass, because they have respectively a historic and prospective relationship to paid employment. In Chapter 2, Nick Buck implements this definition, using households rather than family units because of limitations in the data. In one version, he classifies households according to the activity status of the head; in another, according to the status of the more active of the two partners in couple households. He starts by identifying inactive and long-term unemployed households, then excludes individuals who are not of working age, those who have retired early, people who have a long-term illness and students. The logic of excluding some of these groups can certainly be challenged, but this definition provides a useful starting point.

On this basis, he finds that in 1979, the underclass amounted to 1.96 million people, or 4.2 per cent of the total population in working age households; but by 1986, at the peak of the recession, this had grown to 4.58 million people, or 9.9 per cent of the population in working age households. In 1979, lone parents accounted for 56 per cent of underclass households, couples for 25 per cent, and single-person households for 20 per cent. Between 1979 and 1986, the growth in the number of lone-parent households belonging to the underclass was small compared with the growth of the other types; consequently, in 1986, lone-parent households accounted for 29 per cent of underclass households, compared with 56 per cent seven years before.[1] Groups which were more likely than average to belong to the underclass were local authority tenants, those with no educational qualifications, the youngest and oldest age groups (within the span of working age), families of West Indian origin, and families with large numbers of children. The strongest of these effects was tenure.

A point which is brought out by Nick Buck, and re-emphasised by Anthony Heath, is that it is unclear, as yet, how far the group identified by this analysis, and provisionally labelled 'the underclass', is a stable and persisting one. Between 1973 and 1983 there was a steep and sustained rise in the rate of unemployment in all OECD countries. In most of these countries (Britain included), the rate of unemployment remained on a high plateau throughout most of the 1980s, though in a few it fell much more quickly towards its earlier level. As the aggregate rate of unemployment rose, so the long-term unemployed (those out of work for a year or more) formed an increasing proportion of all the unemployed. Hence, in most OECD countries, the 1980s began a new era of high and persistent unemployment along with rapid growth in the number of people unemployed for long periods.

As Anthony Heath points out, career history data are needed to explore this issue more fully, but it is probable that in the 1980s the majority of the long-term unemployed were not people who had had no stable relationship to work throughout their adult lives. Thus, the group identified by Nick Buck were, in his words 'not so much stable members of an underclass as unstable members of the working class'. However, the future of the underclass as a concept for social analysis depends on the future of the underclass itself. If high unemployment continues indefinitely, then those who have already experienced long-term unemployment are likely to have an increasingly stable experience of detachment from the labour market. As Nick Buck points out, experience of unemployment reduces the prospects of obtaining jobs in the future, both because the individual loses currently relevant skills, and because of employers' selection strategies. If the aggregate level of unemployment persists at a high level over long periods, there will therefore be increasing polarisation between those within and those detached from the labour market, and a declining level of exchange between the two groups. On this analysis, an underclass may not yet exist, but persisting high unemployment may be in the process of creating one.

The culture of the underclass
Three of the contributors – Ralf Dahrendorf, David Willetts, and David Green – assume that the underclass belongs to a distinctive culture which is threatening to mainstream values. According to Ralf Dahrendorf:

> If they [the official classes in advanced societies] are rich enough and have arrangements like the Federal Republic of Germany, they can feed the underclass and not bother about the fact that they are not a part of the labour market or indeed may not be a part of political or social life in general. At the same time, it seems to me that tolerating a group of people for whom this is true, while professing values like those of work or the family, means that one tolerates a not insignificant group which has no stake in the accepted general values... and the values themselves begin to become much more tenuous and precarious than is sustainable for any length of time.

And again, a little later: 'the underclass is the living doubt in the prevailing values which will eat into the texture of the societies in which we are living'.

In the light of such statements, Anthony Heath's findings may come as a surprise. From analysis of surveys carried out in 1987 and 1989, he finds that there is no clear-cut contrast between the attitudes of the underclass and of mainstream society towards children and the family. Some of the results suggest that members of the underclass are likely to place a higher value on children than members of employed family units. At the same time, members of the underclass are likely to have more positive attitudes towards single parenthood than others. None of these differences is large. Members of the underclass are much more likely to want a paid job now than are non-employed members of employed family units. Turnout at the last general election, and feelings of political efficacy, tended to be lower among members of the underclass than among others, but the differences were fairly small.

It is difficult indeed to reconcile these findings with the view that the group provisionally labelled as the underclass is characterised by a highly distinct culture of dependency, which places a low value on work and the family. These findings suggest that theories which see the growth of an underclass as primarily a cultural phenomenon are not grounded in reality. Theories of the underclass should make clear the direction of causation that they propose. One kind of theory is that a change of values among one section of the population – or a moral decline, if we are to use the language of David Green – causes people to withdraw from the labour market. An entirely different theory is that a group which has been mostly out of work for a long period will start to change its values as a consequence. Anthony Heath's findings, along with a great deal of other evidence, makes the first type of theory hard or impossible to sustain. The second type of theory remains plausible.

The determinants of unemployment

Although all developed countries experienced a sharp rise in unemployment from 1973, there are striking differences between countries in the speed with which unemployment returned towards its earlier level. There are also striking differences in the rate of unemployment between different groups, according to age, qualifications, and previous occupation. From the work of economists, sociologists, and political scientists devoted to explaining these differences, it is clear that the institutional and economic factors are the important ones.[2] For example, there is strong evidence from international comparative research that the central reason for the divergence between high- and low-unemployment countries is wage rigidity: the failure of wages in the high-unemployment countries to adjust downwards quickly to compensate for a sudden increase in aggregate unemployment. The UK has shown an exceptionally high level of wage rigidity coupled with an exceptionally large rise in unemployment. One reason for this is that British employers have pursued a strategy of using wage incentives to smooth the path for shedding labour as a simple method of increasing productivity through work intensification. Analyses such as this, which are now securely based on a large body of international comparative evidence, are capable of showing that the aggregate level of unemployment is determined largely by the structure, policy, and practices of institutions, and not by the attitudes of the potential labour force.

The arguments put forward by David Willetts and by David Green rely heavily on the assumption that the aggregate level of unemployment is strongly influenced by the structure of the social security system. However, evidence from comparative analysis of social security systems and unemployment rates in different countries does not support this theory. The OECD has recently published the results of a comparative study of this kind covering 17 industrialised countries.[3] There is found to be no correlation between a country's total unemployment rate and replacement rate (the proportion of earnings replaced by social security payments). Indeed, in the UK, between 1978 and 1988, the period of persistent high unemployment, average benefits for unemployed people fell by about 5 per cent in real terms while average real wages increased by about 40 per cent.[4] Furthermore, unemployed people in the UK appear to have only the weakest adherence to reservation wages, and display considerable persistence in job search and flexibility in accepting low-paid jobs.[5] At the same time there is some relationship between the nature of the social security system and the *structure* of unemployment; and this supports the argument that some features of the social security system may unhelpfully tend to concentrate unemployment among certain groups. For example, there are strong indications from cohort studies of the unemployed in the UK that the benefit system encourages wives whose husbands have been unemployed for a long period to give up their own jobs, because their earnings are counted against their husband's benefit. Thus, the design of the benefit system can reinforce the tendency for unemployment to be concentrated in households, without influencing the aggregate level of unemployment.

Formation of an underclass as a consequence of persistent unemployment

The growth of an underclass must be closely related to the growth of persistent and long-term unemployment. There is now a great weight of evidence to show that persistent unemployment arises from structural and institutional factors and not from the aspirations or attitudes of those who are most at risk.

It remains possible that one consequence of persistent high unemployment will be the formation of an underclass, and there is evidence to suggest that this is likely to happen: evidence, for example, that the unemployed tend to become isolated from contact with people in employment. The data are from the Social Change and Economic Life Initiative (SCELI), which included interviews in 1986/7 with unemployed, employed, and inactive people in six British localities.[6] The results show that the unemployed were less likely than the employed to engage in leisure activities with people outside their own households. As the duration of unemployment increases, the pattern of sociability declines, then increases again, particularly among women. This suggests that there may be some process of adaptation to unemployment among the long-term unemployed. Women are more likely to make this adaptation than men, perhaps because of their distinctive patterns of sociability (which rely more heavily on neighbourly visiting) and because of a lower stigma attached to women being without work.

As well as being less sociable, the unemployed also have different social networks from the employed. The social networks of those in employment consist primarily of others in employment, whereas among the unemployed, but particularly among unemployed men, contact with people in employment sharply declines to a low level as the duration of unemployment increases. Unemployed people, in Gallie's words,

> found themselves increasingly cut off from an effective support system that could help them meet financial difficulties, that could give psychological support and that could provide the information about jobs that was needed if people were to escape from the condition of unemployment. Changes in the pattern of sociability therefore increasingly helped to reinforce their exclusion from the labour market.

To summarise, the theory that an underclass is being created as a result of spontaneous cultural change, or in response to the structure of the social security system, is in conflict with a considerable weight of evidence. On the other hand, the following account of the formation of an underclass would be consistent with the facts. Persistent high unemployment is a failure of the labour market to adapt to major economic shocks, and this failure arises from the structure of labour market institutions, and from the policies and practices of employers and trade unions. As high unemployment persists, it becomes more and more concentrated in particular families, and among particular groups. In time, these groups become increasingly isolated from contact with employed people and the world of work; they begin to adopt a new style of life; and their culture begins to change as a consequence of their life experience.

The limited evidence so far available suggests that any such process cannot yet be far advanced; but it may be in action, and leading to the creation in ten or twenty years' time of an underclass largely detached from paid employment, and having an increasingly separate culture and way of life.

The family

Lone parenthood is a successful way of life for some mothers, particularly those with high earnings or free child care arrangements. On the proposed definition, not all lone parents belong to the underclass, but many do. An interesting feature of Nick Buck's results is that as unemployment rose between 1979 and 1986, although lone parents increased in numbers, they came to form a decreasing proportion of the group provisionally labelled as the underclass. Nevertheless, in 1986 they still accounted for 29 per cent of underclass households. An important element of resistance to the idea of an underclass springs from a desire not to stigmatise lone parents. This is a matter on which there are very sharp differences of opinion. At one extreme there is David Green's view that the welfare of children, mothers, and of the economy is dependent on maintaining, or perhaps re-creating, the family as the main building block of the economy and society. At the other extreme there is the view, implicit in some contributions, but never fully spelt out, that the family is an oppressive institution that places women in a position of dependency, and the main site of male violence towards women and children. Somewhere in the middle, there is the view of the Institute for Public Policy Research that patterns of family life are changing whether we like it or not, and that public policy should adapt to families as they are, rather than try to change them to something different.

The proposed minimalist definition of the underclass, in terms of detachment from the labour market, assumes that the traditional family is the norm. The definition makes use of the idea of family units. On the proposed definition, non-working women with working husbands do not fall within the underclass, because their family unit is integrated into the labour market. On the other hand, non-working lone mothers do normally fall within the underclass. This seems to imply that detachment from the labour market is problematic in the case of lone mothers, but not in the case of wives. Insofar as the underclass is regarded as deviant, the definition therefore implies endorsement of the family based on a couple. The justification for this endorsement, David Green suggests, is the importance of child-rearing: the couple household with children is an economic and social unit in which one partner specialises in child-rearing while the other specialises in paid employment, so the whole unit is attached to the labour market but also adapted to looking after children. Yet if the endorsement of the traditional family unit turns on the importance of child-rearing, it is a paradox that lone mothers define themselves out of the underclass only if they get a job instead of devoting themselves to rearing their children. On these grounds it can be argued that even on the minimalist definition, the idea of an underclass does stigmatise lone parents. They are given a choice between two evils: staying at home to look after their children, in which case they become part of an underclass; or going out to work, in which case they are failing to sustain an ideal of motherhood that others seek to impose.

This discussion does bring out the implications of taking the family unit as the basis for a definition of the underclass, but no other approach seems feasible. It is not the idea of an underclass but existing social and economic structures which impose the paradigm of the family based on a couple. The primacy of work as a source of income, social contact, and social role is well illustrated by the extensive research evidence on the consequences of unemployment. The primacy of work is closely related to the continuance of couple families as the norm, because these families provide economic units within which earnings from employment are distributed more widely to people who are not in employment. Young people raising families require substantial resources if they are not to be struggling in poverty and isolation. If they split off into units of a single adult with a number of children, then they will not under present arrangements generally have enough resources to avoid poverty; and they will be forced into a choice between going out to work with inadequate child care arrangements (because they cannot afford adequate ones) or staying at home with inadequate resources to sustain a reasonable standard of living. This flows not from the idea of an underclass, or from any particular definition of the idea, but from existing social and economic structures, in which the norm is for income from employment to be redistributed within families. It is worth noting that the continuance of the family, in this sense, does not imply that traditional male and female roles have to be immutable: paid work and child-rearing duties could be shared out differently between men and women within the family unit, and of course in some families this has already happened.

On this analysis, the future of the underclass is closely bound up with the future of the family. David Green's recommendation is to restore the couple family by reducing benefits payable to lone parents. Confining the discussion to practical as distinct from moral issues, the problem with this is that the growth in the number of lone parents cannot be primarily a response to economic opportunities, since, even before David Green's proposed reductions in benefit, lone parents tend to be far poorer than couple parents. It is plain that a deep-seated cultural change of some kind is taking place. State benefits enable people to subsist as lone parents, but they do not currently provide an incentive for adopting this style of life.

James Cornford's recommendation is (very broadly) to increase the benefits payable to lone parents and to provide greatly improved child-minding facilities. In general, the problem with this kind of programme is that it may provide an incentive for people to become lone parents. Some benefit changes that are helpful to lone parents are already taking place at the margins. For example, changes in the rules governing Family Credit are allowing an increasing number of lone parents to manage on earnings from part-time work supplemented by benefit. But more radical increases in benefits payable to lone parents could support and even encourage a cultural change that is unsustainable in the longer term. A steep and continuing increase in the number of lone parents, combined with an increase in benefits payable to them, would mean a large increase in the proportion of income that is re-distributed by the state through bureaucratic procedures. Without much wider and deeper changes in societal structures and values, particularly in the primacy of work as the criterion of economic and social worth, such a policy would be sustainable neither fiscally nor politically in the longer term. The policy of creating much better child-minding facilities so that lone parents can take jobs seems more viable, but it creates the need for many more jobs, as it implies a substantial increase in the proportion of the population who are economically active. Of course, single parenthood is already a viable and positive style of life for some, especially those with a high earning potential. The economic disincentive is weakest for those with low potential earnings, yet they are the ones who will suffer most from being lone parents.

What is lacking from both of these prescriptions is any positive, dynamic vision of the future of the family. On the one hand, the Institute for Economic Affairs is trying to put the toothpaste back into the tube, ignoring the tensions and dissatisfactions with the family which are causing it to change. On the other hand, the Institute for Public Policy Research is helping lone mothers to make the best of a bad job, without wishing to endorse the style of life they have adopted.

The idea of an underclass is tied to family units of some kind: that is private associations of people who share resources and tasks (even if they don't share them fairly). It is not, however, tied to any particular paradigm of family structure. Family structures are, in fact, changing. The future of the underclass depends, among other things, on whether they change in a way that avoids the expansion of the group of isolated, workless, lone parents. Perhaps the family is capable of developing in more interesting and progressive ways than any that have been thought of yet.

Ecology
Particular emphasis has been placed on the degeneration of communities is American inner cities because of the exodus to the suburbs of the black middle class. Broadly speaking neighbourhood differences, for example in ethnic composition or crime rate, are starker and more sharply defined in the US than in Britain. Nevertheless, even in the US, as James Cornford points out in an important endnote, most poor and unemployed people live outside the areas of high poverty and unemployment. There is little information, as yet, on the detailed distribution of the underclass in Britain. However, an important finding from Nick Buck's analysis is that the people most likely to belong to the underclass are local authority tenants: this is a stronger predictor than social class or level of education. Since many local authority properties are grouped together on estates, an important question is whether this is partly a spatial effect. It may be one consequence of giving council tenants the right to buy their flats and houses. As the more prosperous tenants on the better estates buy their houses, the remaining stock, which is concentrated in run-down estates, is increasingly confined to groups like the long-term unemployed and lone parents. As this process continues, British council housing becomes more like American 'welfare housing', and similarly stigmatised. In these residual areas of council housing, the social structure may tend to deteriorate, as it does in certain inner city areas in the USA. Analysis of the British Crime Survey reveals that certain types of local authority housing estate (classified in socio-demographic terms) have extraordinarily high crime rates. Future research should aim to establish whether high crime is just one symptom of a wider problem connected with an exceptionally high concentration of the underclass on certain types of local authority housing estate.

The future of employment
The future of the underclass depends on changes in the family, but most of all it depends on the future of employment. The question is whether in the conditions of technical change and competition that will apply over the next 20 years the economy can generate enough new jobs to reduce the high unemployment that has persisted for the last 10 years. That depends on a wide range of economic, institutional, and political factors that cannot be reviewed here. What is highlighted by the underclass discussion, however, is that there must either be effective policies for reducing and eventually abolishing unemployment; or there must be a reduction in the primacy of employment, so that those who do not have a job are not permanently dispossessed of everything that society counts valuable. Persistent high unemployment may not be a viable structure in the long term.

There are observable long-term changes in the structure of the labour market which tend to increase the polarisation captured by the underclass idea. For example, there is probably an increase in the salience of educational qualifications as a determinant of employment prospects, and a decline in the opportunities available to those without skills or qualifications. While British educational standards have probably not declined in absolute terms, they have declined relatively to those in countries such as Germany and France, particularly at the lower end of the ability range. Hence educational and labour market trends in combination may be leading to the creation of a substantial group of young people without marketable skills.

Conclusion

It has not yet been shown that the underclass is a coherent explanatory idea in Britain, but it may turn out to be a good way of explaining the society that will be created by present conditions if they persist. There is a good case for research that aims to understand how to prevent that future from taking shape.

Notes

1. These figures are based on Nick Buck's 'joint activity' classification, not on the classification by the activity of the head of household alone.
2. For a review of the extensive evidence on this topic, see M. White, *Against Unemployment* (Policy Studies Institute, London, 1991); and M. White and D.J. Smith, 'The Determinants of Unemployment' in A. Petersen (ed.), *Youth Unemployment* (forthcoming).
3. See OECD, *Employment Outlook* (Paris, 1991) pp. 199-236.
4. A. Atkinson and J. Mickelwright, 'Turning the Screw: Benefits for the Unemployed 1978-88', in A. Dilnot and I. Walker (eds), *The Economics of Social Security* (Oxford University Press, 1989).
5. See W.W. Daniel, *The Unemployed Flow* (London, Policy Studies Institute, 1990); W. Narendranathan and S. Nickell, 'Modelling the Process of Job Search', in S. Nickell, W. Narendranathan, J. Stern and J. Garcia, *The Nature of Unemployment in Britain* (Oxford University Press, 1989); M. White and S. McRae, *Young Adults and Long-term Unemployment* (London, Policy Studies Institute, 1989).
6. See D. Gallie, 'Social consequences of long-term unemployment' (forthcoming).